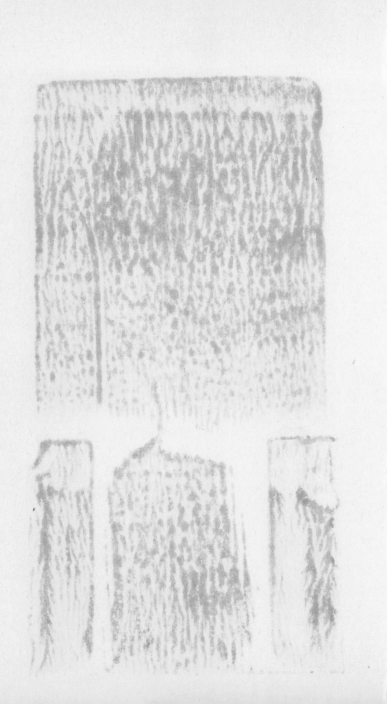

A Baronial Household
of the Thirteenth Century

by the same author

SIMON DE MONTFORT

A Baronial Household
of the Thirteenth Century

MARGARET WADE LABARGE

NEW YORK

BARNES & NOBLE, INC

First published in 1965
© *1965 Margaret Wade Labarge*
Printed in Great Britain by
Billing & Sons Limited
Guildford and London

62431

Contents

5

Plates

Preface

This description of the daily life of a medieval household has been much enriched by the aid of scholars in many different fields who generously shared with me their specialised information. I am particularly grateful to Dr N. Denholm Young, Dr C. H. Knowles, Mr Cook of the Guildhall Museum, Mr Spencer of the London Museum, Mr Lascoe of the British Museum, and Miss Kenway of the Pierpont Morgan Library, New York. Rev. Michael Sheehan CSB, of the Pontifical Institute of Medieval Studies, Toronto, not only allowed me to use his collection of thirteenth century wills, but also provided much valuable criticism of the work in progress. I need hardly say that any remaining errors are entirely my own.

I must express particular thanks to the following librarians and libraries, especially to Miss Ewart of the Ottawa Public Library, and also to the Public Archives of Canada, the Carleton University Library, the University of Ottawa Library, the University of Toronto Library, the Medieval Institute Library, the New York Public Library, the Pierpont Morgan Library, the Public Record Office, the British Museum and the Warburg Institute. Valuable help has come from Mrs Barbara Lambert, Miss Naomi Griffiths, and Mrs Mary Geggie.

Finally, my husband and my own household have been support, sounding-board, and partners in both the enthusiasm and the work caused by this study of a very different pattern of family life, and it is to them that I dedicate it with affection and gratitude.

M. W. L.

Introduction

The everyday life of an earl or great baron in thirteenth-century England has special interest because these men were members of the small elite which ruled England. The pattern of life at this time differed enormously from class to class; indeed, there are almost more dissimilarities than likenesses in the separate routines of an earl or great baron, a knight of the shire, a merchant of the city or a craftsman, or one of the great mass of peasants. Although all knights were theoretically of the same social class, the great baron towered over the simple knight of the shire; he was set apart by his direct link with the king, his greater military resources, his wealth, and his widely distributed lands.

An English earl of the thirteenth century was a prominent member of a military and social aristocracy. Because of the king's need for his counsel and consent in matters which touched the affairs of the realm, and his central role in the levying of the feudal army, he also wielded considerable direct political power. The earls of England were a small group – scarcely a dozen were active at any one time in the thirteenth century. Though they no longer ruled as a matter of course the counties from which they took their titles or wielded the independent power they had exercised in Anglo-Saxon times, they ranked as the most important of all the magnates. Frequently they were very rich men, though few were as wealthy as Richard of Cornwall, Henry III's brother, who had a yearly income of £4,000–£5,000*; or

* It is difficult to give modern equivalents for medieval sums of money. Some idea of the size of these incomes can be achieved by

the Lord Edward, who by 1254 counted an annual £10,000 from his earldom of Chester and his other lands and honours. These particularly high revenues were due to King Henry's desire to see his brother and son suitably enfeoffed, but several of the other earls were also very wealthy. Earl Walter Marshal had £3,350 a year; and Isabella de Fortibus, the heiress to the earldoms of Devon and Aumale, Lady of the Isle of Wight, and the greatest matrimonial prize in England, had an income of £2,500.[1] However, mere wealth was not the only distinguishing feature of an earl's position; his political power and influence depended on several other factors.

Any earl had certain recognized feudal obligations to the king, since he held his earldom directly from the king. Like that of a baron, an earl's tenure was distinguished by the requirement of military service, in person and accompanied by a specified contingent of knights. Originally the obligation to provide this nucleus for the king's army, both for service in campaigns and for castle-guard, had been of overriding importance, since the early feudal army was made up primarily of knights. By the thirteenth century, however, the barons had succeeded in reducing the number of knights whose service they owed to the king, and in fact the king preferred a more reliable body of paid troops. Knights were increasingly used to command considerable numbers of men-at-arms, and the payment of scutage* was common.[2] Another duty of an earl was to give counsel to the king, and to share in the work of the *curia regis*, either in its less formal sessions or in the more general and extensive meetings which were coming to be designated as parliaments. Then too, as

---

comparisons. In the thirteenth century the average unskilled worker received 2d a day, a highly skilled mason, 4d. Even at the upper levels of society, land worth only £20 a year might subject its holder to the royal demand that he be knighted or pay for his freedom from this expensive obligation.

* Scutage was the commutation of military service at a fixed rate, usually £1 or 2 marks (a mark was two-thirds of a £) on the knight's fee.

well as the usual feudal aids, an earl, and also the holder of a barony, owed the king a fixed relief of £100 when he entered upon his inheritance. If he died leaving young heirs, his lands were subject to the king's right of wardship until the heir's coming of age; and the king could also dispose of the marriage of his widow and his daughters.

Some earls might boast a specific title, such as Steward or Marshal, inherited from an ancestor's position as one of the great officials in personal attendance on the king. By the thirteenth century these offices were mainly ceremonial and their duties only formalities. All earls, and many great barons, exercised certain rights of jurisdiction now considered public, and jealously maintained the position and competence of their court. These rights enhanced their power and prestige; they also added to their wealth, since the revenues which came from fines imposed in court, even for such minor matters as infractions of the Assizes of Bread and Ale, were valuable additions to a great magnate's income. These various classes of jurisdiction were specially and specifically granted by the king, and he also allowed to certain earls the privilege of the third penny, that is, the right to one-third of all the revenues from royal justice within the county.

The symbol of the baron's power was the castle which was the head of his honour. An earl, or wealthy baron, would have several castles, usually in different parts of England, and would move his household periodically from one to another. In his capacity as a feudal lord, the earl would demand counsel from his own knights and barons; he would enforce military service or scutage on the knight's fees*

* A knight's fee was a piece of land held in return for the service of one knight, who was bound to render his service equipped with coat of mail, shield, helmet, and lance. The size of these fees was never uniform, but varied widely, and the originally simple scheme had become exceedingly complex by the thirteenth century. Inheritance laws permitted the partition of knight's fees into fractions as small as a

which were held of him. He would levy aids and reliefs, and would claim the right of wardship on his feudal tenants. In addition to these feudal rights, an earl exercised extensive manorial jurisdiction. Some of his manors would be exploited directly through his own officials (and these would be said to be "in demesne") while others were let out to tenants in return for money rents, goods, or services. Even this already complex picture does not include all the sources of profit of an earldom. Any wise magnate would endeavour to contract a financially advantageous marriage, so that he could add to his own scattered holdings strategically situated lands or fees which his wife would bring to their partnership. He might also profit by the occasional windfall of a royal gift or grant, or purchase from the king the wardship of a minor heir to wealthy lands, or the right to dispose of the marriage of a rich widow.

Obviously a thirteenth-century earldom was a combination of many disparate elements, but the pattern of its administrative system, as it developed throughout the century, was flexible enough to deal with the many ramifications. The surviving administrative records not only throw light on the methods used for the management of lands and rents, they also provide welcome information on the affairs and daily routine of the household itself. Unfortunately, there is no one series of documents which deals with both the public and the private affairs of a thirteenth-century earldom or great barony. However the record which throws the most light on domestic life is the household account, the summary made by the steward of the household of daily expenses.

---

twentieth or a hundreth, and great barons had also created more knight's fees within their estates than the service they actually owed to the king. The fractional fees always had to commute their obligation by a money payment, and a royal demand for scutage often provided a baron with a sizeable profit. He collected from all his knight's fees, but only paid the king an amount based on the number of fees for which his honour was assessed.

The earliest of these private household accounts, one which covers seven months of the year 1265, is that of the countess of Leicester.[1] Because of this extraordinarily informative document, it seems suitable to use the household of the earl and countess of Leicester as an example and type of the baronial households of their day. The earl and countess's establishment was wealthier and more important than that of the average baron, but it illustrates many common features of the everyday life of the great magnates, both lay and ecclesiastical, of thirteenth-century England.

The earldom of Leicester was neither the oldest nor the most valuable of the English earldoms. In fact the thirteenth-century earldom had declined sharply in value because of the death without male heirs of Robert IV, the last of the Beaumont earls. As a result, after 1204 the earldom of Leicester was divided between Earl Robert's two sisters, Margaret and Amicia; one half thus passed into the possession of Margaret's husband, the earl of Winchester; while the other passed to Amicia's son, Simon de Montfort, leader of the Albigensian Crusade. The half of the Beaumont inheritance which fell to the Montforts included the title of earl of Leicester, the title of Steward of England, the third penny of the county, half of the lands and rents of Earl Robert including the borough of Leicester, and an assessment of sixty and a fraction knight's fees. The revenues of this half were not high – in 1207 they amounted to only £256.[2]

Simon the Crusader never received full seisin – the feudal lawyer's term for possession – of his inheritance, and for the first third of the century his share of the earldom was in the hands of the king or granted to the earl of Chester. In 1230 the Crusader's younger son, also called Simon, came to England to exploit his rather tenuous claim to the earldom. He was remarkably successful. Henry III, always attracted by foreign adventurers, befriended the young Frenchman, invested him with the earldom, and even countenanced his marriage to Eleanor, the youngest of the royal sisters. Simon's position as earl of Leicester, and even more his exceedingly fortunate marriage, ensured him wealth and prestige, and placed him at once among the leading barons of England.

No convenient list survives of the lands of the earldom which Simon de Montfort received in 1231, and with which he was formally invested in 1239. But in essence his inheritance included those items mentioned in the partition made after Earl Robert's death. The earldom seems to have been even less valuable than it was at the time of Simon the Crusader's claim, for one of Earl Simon's later bitter complaints against the king was that his lands had been badly mismanaged by the royal bailiffs "with great destruction of the woods, and other great damages".[1] Whether or not Simon's statement was true, there is no doubt that the Leicester earldom was not a very wealthy lordship.

Yet Earl Simon took many of his revenues from royal grants and concessions which were not an intrinsic part of his earldom. Thus the king granted the earl and countess the royal castles of Kenilworth and Odiham,[2] and Kenilworth particularly was an important and powerful stronghold. In 1245 the earl profited by the grant of the wardship of the heir of Gilbert of Umfravill, a wealthy northern baron.[3] As the infant heir was only one year old, and the right of wardship which was worth 500 marks a year continued until he reached twenty-one, this was a rich gift. In addition the Countess Eleanor brought to her second husband her dower claims against the heirs of Earl William Marshal to whom she had been married at the age of nine – she was a widow at sixteen. A widow's dower was supposed to be one-third of her husband's estates, which she had the right to hold as long as she lived despite remarriage. Eleanor's claims were a matter of litigation for years, but she finally received £400 a year for her dower lands in Ireland and something over £400 from her dower lands in England.[4] The combination of these many diverse revenues gave the earl and countess

14

of Leicester a considerable income, though like most other members of the baronage they were always short of ready money and usually in debt to either the king or the money-lenders.

Simon de Montfort's early years as earl of Leicester followed the customary pattern of English baronial life. He went on crusade, and returning from this rather unimpressive expedition served King Henry in his unsuccessful Poitevin campaign of 1242. Once back in England, the earl moved from one to another of his castles or manors, frequently forming part of the king's entourage. For several years his growing political importance and his missions for the king were characteristic of his class. A term as king's lieutenant in Gascony, and the difficult task of negotiating the peace with France which culminated in the treaty of Paris of 1259, ensured Simon's recognition as a leader among the baronage. The year 1258 marked the dramatic confrontation of King Henry and his barons over the vital issue of the proper government of the realm. During the next few years England slipped steadily towards civil war, and Simon de Montfort ultimately emerged as the undisputed head of the baronial faction. After the defeat and capture of the king at Lewes, Earl Simon ruled England until his own defeat and death at Evesham in August 1265.

But a study of daily life is not concerned with Earl Simon's extraordinary political position; rather it looks for the features of his household which mirror the general pattern of life among all the great barons. The countess of Leicester's household account is interesting, not so much because it covers this period of upheaval, although this is reflected in the sober language of its entries, but because it typifies the careful accounting system characteristic of every large household. It illustrates most vividly how the steady round of household administration followed a fixed routine, even in a time of civil war and catastrophe. What the countess's household roll tells us about her own establishment may be taken as typical of the other great baronial households of the time.

Other contemporary evidence can help to add depth and meaning to the bare entries on the countess's roll. There are a few other household rolls for the remainder of the century, often fragmentary but always illuminating, though most of them deal with the rather specialized households of the king's children or those of important clerics. Contemporary treatises on estate management are almost as informative as the accounts, and lay down the accepted rules for the various officials. Thirteenth-century treatises on etiquette describe the social customs and general outlook of the time.

Much other incidental information on everyday ways and habits is to be found in less obvious works. Sermons and penitential manuals, prepared to aid in the examination of conscience, reflect current social conditions as they inveigh against men's evil habits or tell stories to point their morals. Grammarians include lists of belongings and foods in their vocabularies, and compilers of encyclopaedic treatises occasionally embellish their frequent quotations from authorities with personal knowledge and experience. Contemporary wills and inventories, too, often describe in loving detail their owner's most valuable possessions and clothes.

In addition to these unofficial sources, certain royal records mirror the everyday affairs of their time. The rolls which summarize the court cases, despite their unfamiliar form, have all the immediacy and personal detail of a modern court transcript. The Liberate Rolls, the record of writs warranting or ordering expenditure, are particularly informative for the reign of Henry III. They are filled with detailed descriptions of buildings, clothes, and jewels; they list the cost of horses and falcons, and account for the payments to servants and chaplains, as well as mentioning their extra perquisites. The Liberate Rolls form a convenient basis for comparison with the accounts of the more limited spending of the great barons, and describe the luxuries which the barons also attempted to acquire. Even the artist often served unconsciously as a social reporter, using the clothes and physical background of his own day in his illustrations of the Old Testament or the Trojan war.

Social history, whether in the wide sweep of a general survey or the detailed examination of a single institution such as a thirteenth-century household, is inevitably pieced together as a mosaic. The fragments of evidence, often insignificant in themselves, combine to form an intelligible picture. When all the incidental information from these various sources is added to the factual entries in the Montfort household account, there emerges a reasonably complete and unromanticized portrait of domestic life in a great baronial household of the time.

1

The Castle as a Home

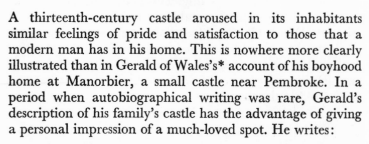

A thirteenth-century castle aroused in its inhabitants similar feelings of pride and satisfaction to those that a modern man has in his home. This is nowhere more clearly illustrated than in Gerald of Wales's* account of his boyhood home at Manorbier, a small castle near Pembroke. In a period when autobiographical writing was rare, Gerald's description of his family's castle has the advantage of giving a personal impression of a much-loved spot. He writes:

> It is excellently well-defended by turrets and bulwarks, and is situated on the summit of a hill, extending on the western side towards the sea-port, having on the northern and southern sides a fine fish-pond under its wall, as conspicuous for its grand appearance, as for the depth of its waters, and a beautiful orchard on the same side, inclosed on one part by a vineyard, and on the other by a wood, remarkable for the projection of its rocks, and the height of its hazel trees. On the right side of the promontory, between the castle and the church, near the site of a very large lake and mill, a rivulet of never-failing water falls through a valley.[1]

Gerald has drawn a delightful picture of the childhood home of which he was so proud, and provided a nostalgic glimpse of the little boy who loved to sit on the promontory overlooking the sea, and watch the ships beating their way from England to Ireland. In its essentials, his sketch underlines the important elements of any small castle of the twelfth or

* Gerald of Wales (c. 1146–1220), of distinguished descent, was archdeacon, courtier and author. His highly personal and prejudiced writings are very important for the history of his time.

thirteenth century which was primarily used as a residence.

Considerations of defence determined the location, design, and construction of a castle. The site was particularly important; by choice, a castle was placed on a piece of rising ground, and anchored on solid rock. Such a situation would make attack as difficult as possible for those besiegers who might hope to achieve its surrender by underground mining. If such a rocky location was not available, or if there was a convenient stream, the castle was partly or wholly surrounded by an extensive body of water, protected as far as possible from any attacker's attempts at drainage. A good supply of fresh water was of prime importance since the stagnant water of many moats was unfit for drinking. Any castle which might have to withstand a long siege also required a good well, preferably carefully protected within the central keep and immune to capture before the final disintegration of the defence.

Warfare in the thirteenth century more often took the form of sieges of strategically important castles than of pitched battles in the open countryside. The art of fortification was more advanced than that of attack, so the advantage normally rested with the defender. When a castle was taken, the cause was usually surrender or treachery, rather than a successful direct offensive. These sieges did not produce the ruins we see today. They were caused by the determination of the king to raze a castle which might disturb the peace of the realm, or by seventeenth-century gunpowder. This destruction has been reinforced by the eroding effects of time, and the frequent tendency of earlier builders to regard dismantled castles as convenient warehouses of cut stone.

The castle as a home varied from century to century. The military architects and historians have described the progressive changes which transformed the simple motte and bailey structure of the period of the Norman Conquest into the highly developed and unified conception exemplified in the great castles of Edward I, such as Caernarvon and

Conway. The mid-thirteenth-century castle had certain special features of its own. About 1250, the castle was not a single structure but a series of separate buildings within a protecting wall. The wall surrounded the whole inside court, or bailey, and served as the first line of the castle's defence. The towers, the wall, and the keep were normally of masonry. The immensely thick walls would be normally faced with whatever stone was obtainable locally, with a filling of rubble – which to a mediaeval mason meant a mixture of stone chips and pebbles bound with mortar.

Space was severely limited within the great stone keep, so accommodation for most of the household activities was provided in numerous wooden buildings erected within the inner courtyard. The kitchen might be an elaborate separate structure or merely a shed protecting the cook and the fires from the weather. Frequently the animals and poultry awaiting their turn for the pot were kept in the courtyard, near the kitchen, till the cook required them. In the bailey was a farriery where the smith shod the many horses needed by the household. A pigeon-loft, often a large and elaborate structure, or a dairy might add yet other varieties of animal life to the courtyard. The bailey might also contain a large chapel for the benefit of all the household, since the small chapel in the keep was normally reserved for the lord and lady of the castle and their immediate retinue. Occasionally another separate building existed to house the bells for the chapel.[1] The general impression is one of a confusing hodgepodge of structures designed for many different uses, but all dominated by the solid masonry of the keep and enclosed by a thick wall.

To add to the confusion, the castle of the mid-thirteenth century was constantly being improved and brought up to date. Henry III thought nothing of erecting an extra chamber and wardrobe, complete with plaster fireplace, for the benefit of a visting bishop and his retinue,[2] and many of the magnates must have ordered construction almost as casually. These small wooden buildings frequently burned down, or had their roofs blown off, and, in any case, have not managed to survive the centuries as have the sturdier stone structures. A series of covered passages might connect the wooden outbuildings to the keep, or to the central hall, and King Henry's instructions give a very prominent place to the building or moving of passages. Indeed the impression that remains of his royal palaces of Windsor or Westminster is one of a great hall entered by a veritable rabbit-warren of corridors, which were changed so often that even seasoned members of the court could easily lose their way.

Although the castle itself was thus subject to change, the peripatetic pattern of life of the king and great barons also called for frequent moves from one castle or manor to another. The magnates would often join the king in his progress from castle to hunting-lodge or favourite shrine. They themselves moved from one stronghold to another as the affairs of their estates or their domestic needs seemed to dictate, so that a baronial household could feel equally at home in a number of different places.

It is difficult to visualize accurately the former exterior of a castle; our reconstructions are too frequently influenced by the existing patina of age and romantic association, which is totally irrelevant. We are startled by Bishop Grosseteste's selection of green, blue, and red as the proper colours of the ideal castle.[1] These colours, of course, were chosen by the bishop for their allegorical and symbolic meaning, but Henry III's orders for decoration make it clear that external whitewash was routine. A fifteenth-century illumination shows the Tower of London as it must also have appeared two centuries earlier, with the White Tower resplendently white dominating the grey river and the huddled houses.[2]

Our mental image of a castle not only neglects the colour and the numerous wooden outbuildings; it also overlooks those integral parts of the structure which have disappeared with time. Thus in some castles the staircase which gave entry to the main hall was built on the outside wall, with the main entrance opening directly into the hall at the first floor level. This staircase was usually made of wood and protected by an elaborate porch, or forebuilding, and Kenilworth preserves an example in stone.

Different materials were used for roofing these many separate buildings within the castle wall. The roof of the keep was naturally the most important, and was usually covered with lead, or occasionally with slate. Lead was the best protection, both against fire and the great stones lobbed against a besieged castle by the attackers' machines. However, lead was extremely expensive; in 1267 it cost £100 to roof with lead the dormitory of St Augustine's abbey in Canterbury.[1] The lesser wooden buildings in the bailey of the castle were thatched or shingled. Thatch was the most common and cheapest of the available roofing materials, but was dangerously inflammable. London tried to prohibit its use in the city after each disastrous fire, but from the frequency of the decrees it is obvious that these orders were rarely obeyed. In castles, however, thatch was avoided as far as possible. A practical owner might cut his costs by transferring an outdated roofing material to another less important building. Thus when the castle of Marlborough was being repaired in 1260, the constable was ordered to take the shingle off the roof of the king's great kitchen and cover it with lead; then he was to use the same shingle to cover the roof of the outer chamber in the high tower which had been stripped of thatch.[2] Lead was also used for gutters to carry water off the roofs. Usually these were projecting spouts, but sometimes there were full-length gutters which carried the water down the wall.

The common design for windows called for wooden shutters held in place by an iron bar, but glass windows were becoming a great deal more common throughout the century. King Henry was rapidly extending the use of glass in all the royal establishments, and the barons who stayed in his castles would have quickly recognized its advantages. In fact, glass windows were rather more common and cheaper in the thirteenth century than is generally recognized. The usual rate for white glass was 4d a square foot, not exorbitant for a man of substance or a great baron. At the end of the century, Bogo de Clare, brother of the rich earl of Gloucester, bought two glass windows, with all their iron work, for only 2s 1d.[1] Richard Swinfield, bishop of Hereford, put a glass window into the chamber of his manor at Bosbury in 1290, at a cost of 6s 8d[2] – further proof of a widespread use of glass in even less important houses. Of course, the use of glass had been common in churches for some time, and was beginning to be required by the canons. An early maintenance contract dates back to 1240. It witnesses to an agreement between a local glazier and the dean and chapter of Chichester whereby, for a yearly fee of 13s 4d and a daily allowance of bread and beer throughout the year, the glazier and his heirs promised to wash, clean, and repair the windows of the cathedral.[3]

These orders for roofing and windows illustrate the baron's desire to keep a castle or manor in good repair and with the current conveniences. Accounts were kept of the necessary building and repairs, and these were charged against the revenues of the castle or manor. New houses and outbuildings were often added for greater convenience and elegance. The more specialized building work was performed by hired artisans, and there are many references to carpenters, plasterers, masons, and tilers, who were paid a daily wage. The semi-skilled workman could probably be hired locally, but the masons, the most skilled of all craftsmen, normally moved around the country to those places where their services were needed at the time. In fact, there even seems to have been a recognized use of outside labour for house-cleaning when this called for unusual efforts. In Bogo de Clare's account the final entry dealing with the construction of his new chamber and wardrobe in London echoes the perennial concern of the tidy householder: "For cleaning house after the departure of the aforesaid masons, tilers, plasterers, and carpenters, 1od." [1] The dirt must have been piled high, for the sum is equivalent to a day's wages for five men.

Inside the great keep of the castle was the required minimum of living-space: a great hall, provision in the basement for supplies, a private chamber, and perhaps a solar, for the lord and lady, a chapel, a well, and privies. In large castles, the number of chambers and guardrooms would of course be multiplied to provide for a larger garrison, as well as for the household. The great hall was the centre of all social activity and the common meeting place. It usually occupied almost the full expanse of the main floor, with a dais at one end, a fireplace in one wall, and screens or "spurs" to block the draughts of cold air from the entry doors. The bed-chamber of the lord of the castle and his wife was normally on the floor above the great hall and provided a relatively private spot.

Every castle had a chapel and a chaplain, since daily mass was the recognized beginning of the day. Attendance at mass was not restricted to the devout, but was a generally accepted obligation, though it was more commonly fulfilled by mere physical presence. The specially pious might hear several masses, but most barons and their households would find a rapidly muttered low mass quite sufficient to satisfy their consciences on ordinary weekdays.

The wardrobe was the castle's storage room where costly spices, cloth, jewels, and plate were stored in chests under lock and key. Although the wardrobe was usually one large room, the term was also applied to a whole series of rooms which made space for the tailoring of the household's robes, as well as for storage. Its place was not fixed, and the essentially flexible nature of medieval domestic architecture is clearly illustrated by the varying locations of the king's wardrobes. Thus in February 1244 orders were sent to the bailiff of the royal manor of Havering to make certain

1. Dover Castle: the ramparts and Constable Tower

2. Entries from the third membrane of Eleanor de Montfort's household roll. The first two entries have been transcribed and translated opposite.

Transcription of first two entries on photograph

Computatum cum Roberto de Westmol' die sabbati post pascham pro c.xix. lb. cere receptis apud Walingeford ante Natale c.xvi.s. Pro lx.lb. amygdalorum xii.s. vi.d. Pro vi.lb. zingiberi (galingal' crossed out) xv.s. Pro viii.lb. piperis xviii.s. viii.d. Pro vi.lb. canelle vi.s. Pro i.lb. croci xiiii.s. Pro i.lb. gariofili xiiii.s. Pro xii.lb. zucari xii.s. Pro vi.lb. albi pulveris cum macis vi.s. Pro i. buxa gingibrade ii.s. iiii.d. Pro pouches et coriis vi.d. Ista capta fuerunt ante Natale per Colinum Cissorem. Item pro iiii.lb. gingibrade per Ricardum Gobion xii.s. Pro xi.lb. et dimidium zucari et x.lb. rise per W. Clericum ante carniprivium xv.s. iii.d. Item per Colinum Cissorem ad Purificationem pro viii.lb. piperis viii.s. Pro vi.lb. zingiberi viii.s. Pro canevacio iiii.d. Pro xx.lb. amygdalorum iiii.s. ii.d. Pro i.quart. croci iii.s. Pro dimid. lb. citoaldi ii.s. per W. Clericum.

Summa xiii.lb. x.s. ix.d. qui debentur eidem Roberto per talliam.

Liberate de garderoba ad coquinam xv.lb. rise. Pro fratribus viii.lb. amygdalorum. Pro capella ab adventu comitisse usque octavas pasche viii.lb. cere. Pro hospitio usque ad idem tempus xxxviii.lb. Liberate domino Almarico in Octabis Pasche liiii.lb. cere et liii.lb. Alem'. Pro cariagio i.dolii vini cere et amygdalorum de Porecestria usque Odiham vii.s. Pro expensis W. Clerici euntis ibidem iii.d. Pro lectis Boletti per dimidiam quadragesimam iii.d.

Summa. vii.s. vi.d.

Translation

Reckoned with Robert of Westmol' on the Saturday after Easter for 119 lbs. of wax received at Wallingford before Christmas, 116s. For 60 lbs. of almonds, 12s 6d. For 6 lbs of ginger (galingale crossed out) 15s. For 8 lbs of pepper, 18s 8d. For 6 lbs of cinnamon, 6s. For 1 lb. of saffron, 14s. For 1 lb of cloves, 14s. For 12 lbs of sugar, 12s. For 6 lbs of powdered sugar with mace, 6s. For 1 box of gingerbread, 2s 4d. For bags and straps, 6d. These were taken before Christmas by Colin the Tailor. Item, for 4 lbs of gingerbread, by Richard Gobion, 12s. For 11½ lbs of sugar and 10 lbs. of rice, by W. the Clerk before Septuagesima, 15s 3d. Item, by Colin the Tailor at the Purification, for 8 lbs of pepper, 8s. For 6 lbs of ginger, 8s. For canvas, 4d. For 20 lbs of almonds, 4s 2d. For ¼ (lb?) of saffron, 3s. For ½ lb of zedoary, 2s, by W. the Clerk.

Sum £13 10s. 9d owing to the same Robert by tally.

Delivered from the wardrobe to the kitchen, 15 lbs of rice. For the friars, 8 lbs. of almonds. For the chapel, from the arrival of the Countess to the octave of Easter, 8 lbs. of wax. For the household during the same time, 38 lbs. Delivered to Sir Amaury on the octave of Easter, 54 lbs. of wax and 54 lbs. of alem(?). For the carriage of 1 tun of wine, of wax and of almonds from Porchester to Odiham, 7s. For the expenses of W. the Clerk going there, 3d. For the beds of Bolettus for half of Lent, 3d.

Sum. 7s 6d.

3. Effigy of Henry III in Westminster Abbey

repairs and changes there, including the lengthening of the queen's privy chamber and the addition of windows so that it might become a wardrobe. Later that year the sheriff of Surrey was ordered to make a fireplace in the king's larder at Guildford, so that "the building can be the queen's wardrobe when she comes there".[1] The wardrobe could even be a separate building, and seems to have been adapted to suit whatever conditions prevailed.

In medieval usage the very word 'wardrobe' is itself open to some misconstruction. The term is sometimes used to describe the privy chamber, or garderobe, for which ample provision was generally made in the castles and larger houses. In many of the castles, as at Kenilworth, there would be a whole tier of privies, one for each floor of the keep. Usually there was a privy chamber off the main bedroom, and frequently there was also one in the wardrobe. These privies were of different types: some emptied directly into the moat that surrounded the castle and, in the case of stagnant water, must have added considerably to the dangers of infection; others were built with drainage shafts ending in a pit, which encouraged odours. Chamber pots were also in use, and the small sums for their purchase are scattered through all the accounts.

Henry III was undoubtedly more sensitive about sanitation than many of his barons, for the Liberate Rolls abound in instructions for the repair, and further construction, of the privy chambers in his castles and manors. The king seems to have been concerned both with the provision of a sufficient number of facilities, and their maintenance in a reasonable condition. Henry's interest in cleanliness and sanitation was one of his notable characteristics, and practicality as well as a desire for beauty marked his building instructions. Thus, in 1260 he arranged for a special conduit to be made to carry off to the Thames the filth from the king's kitchen at Westminster, because of "the stench of the dirty water carried through the halls".[2]

Personal cleanliness was also considered by others besides the king, though few could afford the elaborate plumbing arrangements of royalty by which water was piped into a special bathroom both at Westminster and at Windsor. Most barons and their families bathed in a large tub. According to the manuscript illuminations, these tubs were round, fairly deep, and looked rather like half barrels. Water was poured into them while the bather sat inside and washed. This required much extra work for the servants, and a regular sum was paid to those responsible for the heating and carrying of water. In the countess of Leicester's account, baths are mentioned twice at Odiham, and listed at the rate of 2d or 3d.[1] In the account of Henry, King Edward's small son, the women in charge of the bath were paid at the rate of 3d each. Since Henry was sickly, a gallon of wine was added to his bath on Pentecost eve; this was thought to be strengthening, and cost an extra 4d.[2] Although tub baths were only taken occasionally, daily washing in a basin was part of the accepted code of the upper class, and the washing of hands before and after meals was part of the formal routine of service.

The most advanced sanitary arrangements were often to be found in the monasteries, and the monks were very clever in the use of nearby streams. Thus at Leeds (Kent), the monks ingeniously dammed a spring high on the hill to create a fish-pond, routed the stream under the buildings for drainage, and then allowed it to emerge to work the mill.[3] Indeed they even provided refinements which the king himself did not boast. In 1267, the chamberlain of St Augustine's abbey, Canterbury, among other benefactions to the monastery, "built the bathrooms afresh and constructed the baths therein"[4] – a considerable improvement on the barrel-like tubs. Public baths also existed in many towns, a fragment of the Roman inheritance still generally used, though not patronized by the magnates. Contrary to modern misconceptions of medieval life, the upper classes particularly took considerable trouble to achieve what they considered a necessary minimum of sanitation. In fact their standards of personal cleanliness were much higher than those which prevailed from the sixteenth to the eighteenth centuries.

Without and within, the castles of the period shared certain general characteristics. The considerable difference between a small castle used primarily as a residence and a large one dominated by strategic requirements is well illustrated by the contrast between Odiham and Dover, the two castles occupied by the countess of Leicester during the period of her household account.

The earl and countess had other castles as well, including Leicester and Kenilworth. Leicester castle was of little importance at this time, although its location was good and it was well protected by the river Soar. Because of the unsuccessful revolt of 1174 in which a previous earl of Leicester had been a leader, King Henry II had ordered the fortifications of this danger spot to be dismantled and the castle sank into obscurity for a century. However the buildings were not destroyed, and the castle was occasionally used as a residence and centre of administration for the earl.[1]

Kenilworth was a gift to Simon de Montfort and Eleanor from Henry III, and after several temporary grants was given to them for life in 1248.[2] The surviving square keep of rosy sandstone gives a very fair idea of the core of the castle in Earl Simon's time. The extraordinary feature of Kenilworth was the magnificent lake that surrounded the castle. The Great Pool, as it was called, covered an area of about one hundred and eleven acres; about a half mile long, it was a hundred yards wide at the south side. Invaluable for defence, the Great Pool also seems to have added to the amenities of the castle. William Dugdale, the seventeenth-century antiquarian and the first historian of Warwickshire, declared that King Henry, in the days before he gave the castle to Simon and Eleanor, kept a boat outside his chamber door for use on the lake.[3] It is a charming picture, though no one has yet been able to find the source of Dugdale's information. In 1265, however, Kenilworth was no longer a residence; it was being used as a base for the baronial military operations, as well as a safe stronghold for such important prisoners as the king's brother, Richard of Cornwall.

Odiham is typical of the smaller, more homely type of castle, and resembled many baronial fortresses. Situated about halfway between the great royal castle of Windsor and King Henry's favourite palace of Winchester, Odiham had been given to Eleanor in 1236, soon after her royal brother's marriage. The original gift included Odiham manor, and the following year Henry added the park and the hunting rights[1] – a valuable privilege since Odiham had been newly built by King John to take advantage of the excellent hunting nearby. Its site was twenty acres of meadow to the north-west of the present town, and the castle was originally only an octagonal tower surrounded by a ditch. As the land was low and marshy the ditch became a natural moat, and had enough fresh water to allow an early custodian of the castle to seek the king's licence to stock it with bream. This convenient fish-pond served as a handy food supply for the many fast days. Only the ruins of the castle now remain, but antiquarians have been able to trace the general outlines of the main tower and its divisions.

The tower consisted of a basement and two upper stories and was about sixty-eight feet high and one hundred and seventy-six feet around. The walls were ten feet thick, so that the interior diameter was only thirty-eight feet – not very large for the number in the household. The basement floor was about six feet below ground level, but the room had a height of twelve feet. It had a few window slits, and an opening for a staircase to the hall above. The great hall occupied all the main floor, rising some thirty feet in height. In the wall of the south face there was a very large fireplace with a hood and mantel of square-cut stone with its circular chimney carried up in the thickness of the wall. Each face of the octagon had a roundheaded arch, about eight feet wide and slightly splayed. These probably narrowed to small coupled windows which provided some light and air. In many surviving examples of the time, the space below the windows was slightly cut away to make window seats. Such niches helped to solve the seating problem when the benches had been removed after meals, or when individuals sought a private conversation. On the upper floor, the one room seems to have been a smaller replica of the great hall below. It was only about eighteen feet high, but it too had window recesses, and another small fireplace opening on the main chimney shaft. The floors of these two stories were of timber, heavy beams which radiated from a supporting centre post.[1]

So much surviving ruins can tell the experienced investigator, and his deductions can be supplemented by contemporary records which occasionally mention less permanent outbuildings that normally clustered round the central keep. In 1239 the king ordered one of his men to complete the kitchen at Odiham which Simon de Montfort had commenced, and also to see about finding a chaplain to minister to the king's chapel there.[2] These must have been outside buildings as there was no room for them within the tower. A year later, the king had to issue another order for the completion of the hall and kitchen to Paul Piper, who was serving as keeper of the manor of Odiham during the absence overseas of the earl and countess of Leicester. A trusted royal official and king's knight, Piper was also the Montforts' tenant on Eleanor's manor of Toddington. The testimony suggests that he was a rich man with a developed taste for architecture and decoration that much resembled that of the king he served. Matthew Paris tells us that he embellished the manor of Toddington "by building a palace, chambers, and other houses of stone covered with lead, and constructed orchards and warrens there to the admiration of all beholders". It appears to have been an expensive project,

as Matthew adds that "the men who constructed his buildings are said to have been paid 100s a week, and often 10
marks, for several years".[1] Medieval chroniclers are
notoriously unreliable about figures, but 100s a week would
imply a very large group of workmen at the skilled worker's
wage of 4d a day.

Many of the same features which characterized the small
and relatively peaceful castle of Odiham are also to be found
in the great fortress of Dover, but the difference in importance
and emphasis is striking. Dover, perhaps even more than the
Tower of London, was the most important stronghold in
the whole kingdom. Its nickname, 'the key of the realm',
was testimony to its pre-eminence. Firmly planted on the
heights of Dover so as to control the busy harbour, the
strategic spot of the narrow seas, the castle was a superbly
strong fortress. Its commanding position made it a majestic
sight even from a distance. Several centuries later Dorothy
Wordsworth described, in the journal of her French trip,
the castle's domination of the English coastline. As Dorothy
and William walked along the sands near Calais, they saw
"far off in the west the coast of England like a cloud crested
with Dover Castle, which was but like the summit of the
cloud".[2]

Close at hand all cloudlike visions faded against the
massive solidity of its architecture. The great square keep
had been built at the end of the twelfth century and towered
to a height of eighty-three feet, while the square turrets at
the corners rose another twelve feet. The walls were twice
as thick as those at Odiham, averaging about twenty-one
feet. In the forebuilding there were two chapels, one above
the other; probably one was intended for the use of the
garrison and the other for the constable of the castle and his
household, as in the similar arrangement at Sainte Chapelle.
The guardroom was at the head of the flight of stairs in the
forebuilding, facing down the steps – an excellent position
to protect the main entrance against a sudden rush. The

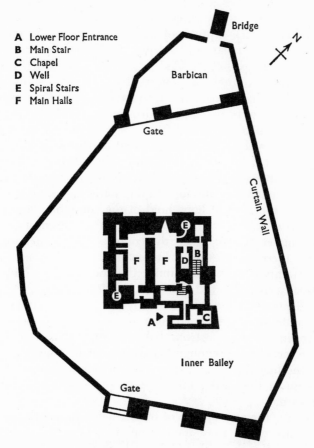

A Lower Floor Entrance
B Main Stair
C Chapel
D Well
E Spiral Stairs
F Main Halls

Dover Castle, showing inner curtain wall, bailey, and main floor of keep. An outer ward was protected by another curtain wall built by Henry III in the early part of his reign.

deep well, which went down two hundred and fifty feet, was in a wall chamber just inside the entrance of the keep. To protect the necessary water supply, there was also a storage tank from which supplies of water were carried to the rest of the keep by means of lead pipe buried in the walls. The keep was completely divided by a cross wall which ran its full height, so that each floor had two long halls. The principal living quarters seem to have been on the top story where there were two large halls, some wall chambers, and an upper gallery all round.[1]

Such a castle had to be prepared and provisioned, even in peacetime, for the coming and going of large numbers. Besides those serving on castle-guard, there would be many visitors, messengers and foreign dignitaries, all adding to the needs of the normal household of the constable. However, the castle's capacity was stretched to the uttermost during the summer of 1265 when the countess of Leicester sought refuge there. Besides her own small household, there were also twenty-nine archers under the command of John La Warre, who reinforced the castle's defences during August and September and were paid by the countess.[2] But when Simon de Montfort the younger accompanied his mother to Dover in July with a strong band of supporters, even Dover castle was not large enough to harbour all this great assembly. For the first three days, the countess, her women, and her son ate in the castle, but their households had to eat in the town.[3]

Despite the atmosphere of bustle, noise, and close-packed humanity which must have been the general condition of Dover castle, there should have been an occasional quiet spot, since in 1256 King Henry was supporting an anchoress there at the comfortable rate of $1\frac{1}{2}$d a day.[4] Unfortunately we have to imagine for ourselves where in that great warren of a building the anchoress found the seclusion and holy privacy which were commanded for recluses. Even so, Dover was not unique in its possession of an anchorite. Twenty years before, a Brother William was described as the recluse of St Peter in the bailey of the Tower of London, and was given 1d daily for his maintenance so long as he remained there.[1] This would seem to be another example of the medieval conviction of the importance of spiritual, as well as military, support.

Many people lived ordinary lives in a castle which served as a home, as well as a stronghold to control or intimidate the surrounding countryside. Since the requirements of daily life presuppose more than the bare shell of the surviving walls, some account has been given of their original functions as halls and chambers, wardrobes and kitchens. But it is impossible to re-create the everyday life of the time without decorating these rooms or filling them with their contemporary furnishings.

The thirteenth century had no aesthetic bias towards undecorated stone, and whitewash was used inside as well as out. The further adornment of inside walls with wainscoting or painting depended both on the wealth and the artistic taste of the individual. King Henry's Liberate Rolls suggest that gallons of green paint and whole galaxies of gold stars and spangles were used on the royal walls during his reign. The rose of Provence, as a delicate compliment to his queen, Eleanor of Provence, also decorated many rooms. By the end of the century there is more frequent evidence of hangings, usually of painted cloth rather than woven tapestry, and also of carpets. The latter were at first considered rather decadent luxuries, and Matthew Paris describes with insular scorn their use in the elegant entourage of the Spanish ambassadors who came to England in 1255.[2]

Furnishings were also sparse. Since life was mainly peripatetic, most of the objects necessary for the comfort of the household had to be carried from place to place in the long strings of carts and pack-horses which were an inescapable part of every move for a great household. This in itself discouraged extensive use of things not easily transported.

The number of items considered as necessities was very modest. John of Garland* listed in his vocabulary the necessary furnishings of an honest man's house, and specified: "a decent table, a clean cloth, hemmed towels, high tripods, strong trestles, firebrands, fuel, logs, stakes, bars, benches, forms, armchairs, wooden frames and chairs made to fold, quilts, bolsters, and cushions".[1] Then he went on to detail all the implements required by a cook, including a perennially useful mouse-trap! He was not talking of the upper classes, but he was anxious to widen the vocabulary of his students and included all the items he knew. Nevertheless, he lists remarkably little of what we would call furniture: much of it would be more accurately described as kitchen equipment or household linen.

The furniture of the thirteenth century was limited to beds in their various forms, and with their accompanying bedding, tables, still normally made of boards placed on trestles, and chairs, or more frequently benches. There were also chests of several sizes, many of which were large enough to be considered as furniture. The chest was usually very sturdily made, bound with iron and closed with lock and key. It was in constant use as a safe depository for any articles of value. Small caskets for jewels were often decorated with ivory or enamel and were very elegant.

The most important single piece of furniture was the great bed of the lord and lady in their chamber. It consisted of a heavy wooden frame, such as John of Garland mentioned, laced with leather thongs or heavy cords, and fitted into sturdy foot and head-pieces. In many cases these frames could be dismantled and transported with the rest of the baggage, but in the homes of the king and some of the great barons they were coming to be permanent and increasingly massive.

* John of Garland was an eminent English scholar living and teaching in France at the beginning of the thirteenth century. His vocabulary was probably written between 1218 and 1229, although he lived until the middle of the century.

On the wooden frame was spread the mattress, preferably of feathers, the sheets, coverlets, and pillows. These were all treasured items which figured regularly in the distribution of goods in contemporary wills. The Countess Eleanor had a particularly handsome set of bedcovers given her by her brother the king on the first Christmas after her marriage to Simon de Montfort. The quilt and mattress were made of the rich and costly baudekin cloth over fustian, and the coverlet was grey fur lined with scarlet – surely a warm combination for a damp winter's day. The cost, including the making and the materials for packing, was well over twenty pounds;[1] it was a splendid gift even for a king to give his sister.

The bed was surrounded by linen hangings, white or coloured, suspended from poles on rings, and pulled back during the day when the bed served as an auxiliary seat. On the walls, wooden 'perches' or long pegs served both as hangers for clothes, and resting places for the ubiquitous birds – the falcons, the hawks, or a domesticated magpie. Apart from a few chests of valuables, a bench or stool, and perhaps a great standing candlestick, there would be no other furniture. A few of the ladies of the household might sleep on truckle beds in the chamber, where the curtains pulled around the great bed gave the lord and lady a measure of privacy. But beds were scarce, and at night the lesser members of the household might well throw a straw pallet or, if they were particularly fortunate, a feather bed, upon a bench in the hall. It was one of the duties incumbent upon the lady of a house to protect the morals of her maidens and female servants and to see that no temptation came their way, so sleeping quarters would be provided for them well away from the men and under the supervision of an older woman. The insignificant grooms merely settled on the rushes of the floor, or burrowed into a convenient spot in the outside straw.

The hall, too, would commonly be furnished very simply.

On the dais, or raised platform, which marked the head of the hall, there would be at least one and possibly two great chairs for the lord and his lady; everyone else sat on benches. As the tables were normally put up for each meal, the board and its supporting trestles would be brought forward when needed and covered with a long white cloth. The cloth was always a matter of considerable pride, and a lord was considered ill-bred whose cloth was dirty or scanty. The greatest, barons, like the king, had permanent tables in some of their castles, but these "dormant" tables, as they were called, were still relatively rare in the thirteenth century. As well as the benches, there were a few folding chairs in wood; known as X-chairs, they were patterned on the curule chairs of Roman days. They seem to have been reserved for the more important members of the household, and for times other than meals. Although the hall was frequently crowded with people, little seating was provided. Most medieval people seem to have thought little of standing for long periods of time or, if younger or of lower status, sitting on the rushes of the floor.

For a thirteenth-century baron life indoors was always a poor substitute for outdoor activity. Despite the great fireplace and the screens blocking the draughts, the hall was frequently damp, dark, and cheerless during the long winter. The high cost of candles and the inefficiency of rush-lights drove most to bed soon after nightfall. Life in winter was only enjoyable when a crowd gathered for a great feast, or when a minstrel's song, and the welcome warmth of the fire, added to the pleasure of supper on a cold evening. Under the prevailing harsh and uncomfortable conditions it is little wonder that the medieval poets, and even the sober chroniclers, sang the joys of spring with such lyric intensity. It gave them back light, warmth, and their freedom of movement.

The castle with its few large rooms, its huddle of outbuildings, and its sparse furniture, was the physical background for the everyday life of a great household such as that of the earl and countess of Leicester. Against this background the countess had to fulfil her special obligations as the lady of the house.

2

The Lady of the House

If it is difficult to think of the castle as a home, it is even
harder to estimate fairly the position of the lady of the house.
The evidence is varied and conflicting. On the one hand,
the moralists and the writers on manners underline the basic,
divinely-ordained subordination of women; they emphasize
their foolishness and the need of their obedient submission
to man in the person of their husbands. On the other, the
romances present the ideas and standards of courtly love;
they describe amazing heroines for whose supercilious smile
any right-minded knight would brave death innumerable
times. But the ladies of the romances generally seem to be
only cardboard figures, cut to an identical pattern. The
description of the heroine of *Jehan et Blonde* illustrates the
accepted type.* Blonde was the ideal heroine with hair of
shining gold, dark, straight eyebrows, and white unwrinkled
skin. Her tiny mouth had full red lips over little white teeth,
and her breath smelt pleasantly sweet. Her throat was so
long and white that the author poetically insisted that you
could see when she drank red wine.[1] The catalogue goes on,

---

* *Jehan et Blonde*, by Philippe de Beaumanoir, was one of the most
popular French romances of the thirteenth century. It has a special
interest for English readers because its central situation, of a French
younger son gaining love and fortune in England, parallels the true life
story of Simon de Montfort. The author probably formed part of Simon's
household for a time, and certainly was familiar with English ways. This
romance was a product of his youth, when he was known as Philippe
de Remi; many years later, as sire de Beaumanoir, he wrote *Coutumes
de Beauvaisis*, the most famous lawbook of thirteenth-century France.

but even this brief sample is sufficient to illustrate the medieval requirements for the fashionable beauty.

Neither the moralists' nor the romancer's descriptions of women had much relation to reality, for the chroniclers quite incidentally provide occasional glimpses of women who did not fit into these stock categories. There was Nicolaa de la Hay, for example, who held the castle of Lincoln for the boy king Henry during the desperate siege of 1216. The redoubtable countess of Arundel, who in 1252 reproved Henry III for his refusal to do justice to his barons and taunted him with his failure to keep his oaths to uphold the Great Charter, was a woman of great force, praised for her outspokenness.[1] Even more impressive was Blanche of Castile, queen and regent of France and the backbone of French administration for a quarter of a century. These women were obviously neither cardboard beauties nor foolish, submissive sheep. Indeed the roster of independent, active and capable women could be greatly extended at many levels of the social scale. Contemporary evidence affords considerable insight into the actual relation of the female stereotype to the reality, and enables us to evaluate more accurately the true place of women in thirteenth-century society.

It must be remembered that there was an enormous gulf between the occupations and status of the young girl and the married woman. At this time fourteen was generally considered the normal marriageable age for a girl. An important heiress, or a royal relative, who served as a pawn in the absorbing game of feudal politics, might be betrothed much earlier. The Countess Eleanor had been married at the age of nine in the hopes of assuring the loyalty of her first husband, Earl William Marshal the younger. Her elder sister Joanna had been betrothed at the age of four, as part of a peace settlement between King John and the Lusignan family of Poitou. Even the less well born unmarried girl was likely to be both young and foolish, and often in need of all the stringent protection the moralists insisted on. The single girl had no real tasks and little social standing; she therefore looked forward to marriage which brought her prestige and an independent establishment. The married woman was charged with the considerable responsibility of directly supervising the affairs of the household. This was particularly true in less extensive establishments than that of the countess of Leicester. The initiative and ability of the wife of a lesser baron were at once more obvious and more necessary.

Apart from her domestic responsibilities, the woman had a recognized legal position; though her lands and goods were theoretically under the control of her husband, she was in fact the equal of a man in all matters of private law. Frederick Maitland, the great legal historian, puts the matter most clearly:

> The woman can hold land, even by military tenure, can own chattels, make a will, make a contract, can sue and be sued. She sues and is sued in person without the interposition of a guardian; she can plead with her own voice if she pleases; indeed – and this is a strong case – a married woman will sometimes appear as her husband's attorney. A widow will often be the guardian of her own children; a lady will often be the guardian of the children of her tenants.[1]

Thus the wife of any great baron would expect to cope with her own property and lands; also to understand and carry on the many legal and financial affairs of the barony during her husband's absence or after his death. Robert Grosseteste, the great bishop of Lincoln, wrote a brief treatise on administration for the countess of Lincoln after her husband's death in 1240.[2] He took for granted her ability to supervise the seignorial and manorial officials, as well as her own immediate household, and merely wrote down some instruction on the accepted methods. The best evidence for the independence and initiative of women is to be found in the numerous court cases in which they figure. Countess Eleanor's legal struggle for her full dower rights, which dragged on for over forty years, is only a particularly long-drawn-out instance of the persistent litigiousness of both sexes in thirteenth-century society.

Obviously the wife of a great baron often played an extraordinarily important part in the marriage partnership. Her varied activities were such an accepted fact that contemporary writers usually ignore them as too ordinary for comment. Nor do they refer to the bond of unity and affection which frequently developed in medieval marriages, even though these were primarily arranged to increase wealth or power. Husband and wife often worked together in a common purpose, and showed a mutual respect which was not echoed by the woman-hating moralists.

Surprisingly these didactic writers seem blinded by their clerical animus, and singularly remote from practical affairs. They pay little attention to the legal and financial responsibilities of a baron's wife, or the important position of middle-class women in many of the town trades. Instead they fall back on the trite statement that a good wife is man's greatest gift from heaven, although they hasten to add that this is only true if she behaves herself and obeys him.

The writers of the treatises on etiquette are equally conventional and uninformative. Stephen of Fougères, chaplain of King Henry II and later bishop of Rennes, had a narrow conception of the proper employments of a great lady. To judge by his praise of the countess of Hereford, the best way for a gentlewoman to occupy her time was in building chapels, decorating altars, caring for the poor, and honouring and serving high personages – to which the bishop thoughtfully added, "especially churchmen".[1] One wonders what he thought of the extremely secular activities of Eleanor of Aquitaine, Henry II's indomitable queen. Fortunately not all the didactic writers were quite so pious, or so limited. Robert of Blois,* for example, breathes a welcome air of

---

* Robert of Blois was a French poet who wrote in the middle of the thirteenth century. His treatise on manners has perhaps some element of satire in it but generally echoes the accepted requirements of the times.

common sense in his discussion of the matter. He admitted that he would like to teach ladies how to behave, but he realized that it was very difficult for a lady to conduct herself well in the world.

If she speaks, someone says it is too much. If she is silent, she is reproached for not knowing how to greet people. If she is friendly and courteous, someone pretends it is for love. If on the other hand she does not put on a bright face, she passes for being too proud.[1]

The problem of contradictory advice to women is obviously not a modern development.

About 1265, Philip of Novara* wrote a little treatise called the *Four Ages of Man* in which he dealt with the proper education of upper-class boys and girls. His work provides convenient clues to what the age expected of them. Philip, like most other medieval writers, emphasized the importance of largess as the prime virtue of kings, princes and the nobility. Generosity could cover a multitude of sins, and any man with pretensions to noble blood must practice it as part of his duty to his class and himself. However, largess was not a suitable virtue for a girl, or even a woman. A maid had no need to make gifts, Philip thought, and he quoted approvingly the common saying, 'poorer than a maid'. His disapproval of gift-giving by married women stemmed from strictly practical reasons:

If the wife and husband are both generous, it is the ruin of the house, while a wife's greater generosity shames her lord. The only kind of largess suitable for a woman is the giving of alms, provided she has her husband's permission and the household can afford it.[2]

In Philip's opinion, obedience and chastity should be a girl's main virtues, and were the only ones strictly required.

* Philip of Novara was a Lombard crusader who settled in the East and wrote a chronicle favourable to the Ibelin family. His treatise on manners was written when he himself was seventy-five.

They were aided by a "fair countenance", that is, the habit of looking straight ahead "with a tranquil and measured air, not too high and not too low, modestly and without affectation".[1] This question of a woman's style of walking and regarding others was one on which all the writers on manners laid great emphasis. Ladies were to walk erect, with dignity, said Robert of Blois, neither trotting nor running, nor dallying either, with their eyes fixed on the ground ahead of them. They were to be particularly careful that they did not regard men as the sparrowhawk does the lark.[2] Anger and high words would also inevitably injure their reputations.

The feminine range of accomplishments was not expected to be very great. Every girl should learn to spin and weave, Philip of Novara insisted, because the poor will need the knowledge and the rich will better appreciate the work of others; but should not be taught to read and write unless she was to become a nun. Many evils, said Philip disapprovingly, have come from the fact that women have learnt such things, for then men dare to write follies or supplications which they would not dare to say or send by messenger.[3] Philip ended his injunctions with the rather patronizing remark that even old women might be useful, for "they can manage and watch their houses, raise the children and arrange marriages". At least, the good ones occupied themselves in these ways, but the bad "plaster their faces, dye their hair, waste their patrimony in seeking love when they are old".[4]

The requirements for the ideal woman put forward by such writers as Robert of Blois and Philip of Novara probably have as much relation to the realities of their time as the formalities of present-day writers on etiquette have to ordinary social life. They mirror the contemporary French ideals of polite behaviour carried to extremes. But, in the thirteenth century too, a good wife was rather more than the bloodless embodiment of the virtues preached by the moralists, or even the competent administrative helpmeet. The Knight of

La Tour Landry, in the prologue of his fourteenth-century book of deportment for his daughters, describes most eloquently the bond of love and respect that bound him to his dead wife. According to the Knight, she was:

> Both fair and good, which had knowledge of all honour, all good, and fair maintaining, and of all good she was bell and the flower; and I delighted so much in her that I made for her love songs, ballads, rondels, virelays, and diverse things in the best wise I could. . . . And so it is more than twenty years that I have been for her full of great sorrow. For a true lover's heart forgetteth never the woman that once he has truly loved.[1]

This was indeed a noble compliment, although perhaps influenced by literary convention. It is a useful counterbalance to the belief that marriage and love were quite incompatible in the Middle Ages.

The countess of Leicester did not altogether conform to the patterns laid down by writers on morals and manners. Her character and activities can afford one example of how thirteenth-century theory about the place of women was carried out in practice. Certainly the countess was no cipher. Eleanor brought Simon de Montfort great wealth, as she was the widow of one of the greatest earls of the realm; also great prestige because she was the king's sister. These two facts alone would have ensured her importance. In addition her character was assertive – she was not the meek, submissive, dove-like type so highly praised by the moralists. Several years earlier, the Franciscan Adam Marsh had found it necessary to write to her reprovingly, suggesting that she lay aside all contentions and irritating quarrels and act in a spirit of moderation when she had to counsel her husband.[2] Obviously a high-spirited woman, she was also unfailingly loyal to Earl Simon through good times and bad. She shared many of her husband's travels – to Italy, France, and Gascony, but she was also capable of handling their many concerns alone. The evidence of the household account shows the countess at a period when she was, of necessity, in charge. The earl was away, engaged on his campaigns, and the management of all their affairs lay in her hands. The role of the countess at this time was more than ever that of the woman of affairs. Even the sober items of the account show how much political initiative Eleanor displayed, and how the executive ability and practical foresight of a capable woman were extended to their furthest limits.

On the domestic side the countess had many officials to take care of the immediate requirements of the household, though she herself had to oversee their accounts and agree to their expenditures. For female companionship she had certain women, who also served as ladies-in-waiting and were referred to as the countess's damsels. Her daughter Eleanor was now almost thirteen, but she still had her own nurse and took an unimportant place in the life of the household.

Indeed the medieval magnates had surprisingly little to do with their children. Almost immediately after birth, they were handed over to the care of a nurse whose duties, as described by Bartholomew the Englishman,* included not only the physical care of the child, but also the display of affection which is now considered essentially maternal. According to Bartholomew the nurse's duties were very extensive. She was ordained to nourish and feed the child, to give it suck, to kiss it if it fell, and comfort it if it wept, and to wash it when it was dirty. The nurse was also to teach the child to speak by sounding out the words for him, to dose him with medicines when necessary, and even to chew the toothless child's meat so that he could swallow it.[1] The mother must have been a rather remote figure. Discipline

* Bartholomew the Englishman was a thirteenth-century Franciscan who wrote an immensely popular encyclopaedia, *Concerning the Nature of Things*. He dealt with a multiplicity of subjects, ranging from the nature of God and the angels to the size of the cooking pots. His work was widely used as a textbook until the sixteenth century.

was always considered the father's primary duty. Bartholomew specifically insisted that the father must treat his child
with harshness and severity. He should teach him with
scoldings and beatings, put him under wardens and tutors,
and, above all, show "no glad cheer lest the child wax
proud".[1] The old adage of "spare the rod and spoil the
child" was firmly entrenched in all medieval treatises on the
proper upbringing of children.

The earl and countess of Leicester had taken care to put
these precepts into practice. In 1265 they had six living
children, ranging in age from twenty-six to thirteen. Two of
their sons had been sent when young to the household of
Bishop Grosseteste to be instructed in good manners and
some learning. It was a recognized medieval practice to send
both boys and girls away to more important or more learned
households as a way of furthering their education. Now the
two eldest boys, Henry and Simon the younger, had been
knighted and were a valued part of their father's army.
Guy was also a fighting man with his father. The fourth son,
Amaury, was a clerk; he had profited handsomely by his
father's success for he had been appointed, at the age of
twenty-one, to the rich office of treasurer of York. Richard,
the youngest of the sons, is a shadowy figure who flits briefly
through the records before his departure for Bigorre in
September when he disappears completely. The only
daughter, Eleanor, remained with her mother during this
period, but her father was busy trying to arrange a marriage
for her with Llywelyn, prince of Wales. Earl Simon hoped
to reinforce the alliance between the baronial troops and the
wild Welsh tribesmen. However, the catastrophe of Evesham
changed all this. Young Eleanor accompanied her mother
into exile in France, and the betrothal to Llywelyn was
postponed. Finally the countess succeeded in having it
carried out by proxy in France just before her death in 1275.
Even then complications of policy forced a further post-
ponement of three years before Eleanor's marriage was

solemnized and, at the age of twenty-six, she was finally free to join her Welsh prince.

It seems to have been the usual practice for each child in an important household to have his own nurse. In the countess's account, besides the payment for young Eleanor's nurse, there is also mention of the nurse of William de Braose.* This multiplicity of nurses is also evident in the household of young Henry, the son of Edward I. There were three children in that household: Henry himself, his elder sister, Eleanor, and their cousin, John of Brittany; each of these children had his own nurse. These ladies were of some standing, since their robes, a considerable addition to their annual wages and a gauge of social position, were of the same value as those of the official guardian of the household.[1] Henry's account also underlines the fact that it was the nurse, not the mother, who was constantly present. The queen sent messengers enquiring after the health of the sickly lad, but affairs of state and the pattern of behaviour of the time kept them apart even in his final illness. The thirteenth century regarded children's deaths as a frequent, and inevitable, example of the inscrutable will of God.

It is obvious that the duties of the countess, or of any great baron's wife, were not restricted to her home and family in the sense in which later centuries have understood these terms. A great magnate's wife was not expected to be a very domestic woman – her duties dealt with a wider sphere. The account shows very clearly two fields in which the countess's personal initiative was particularly important. Eleanor entertained a great number of people, both at Odiham and Dover, during the spring and summer of 1265; she also had an extraordinarily wide range of correspondence.

* William's place in the household remains in doubt. Probably he was a relation of the famous marcher family to which Earl Simon's great-aunt, Countess Loretta of Leicester, belonged, and may have been a hostage for father or uncle, as a William de Braose holding lands in Dorset and Kent was a vigorous loyalist.[2]

Visitors were a common and welcome feature of medieval social life. Indeed one of the primary duties of the gently-born, and especially of the heads of a household, was to greet all their guests with enthusiasm and courtesy. Grosseteste counselled the countess of Lincoln that all guests, secular and religious, should be received "quickly, courteously, and with good cheer", and then they should be "courteously addressed, lodged, and served".[1] It is an interesting peculiarity of the Montfort household account that the clerk each day listed by name those guests of importance who ate with the countess. This gives us valuable clues to the nature of people who came on varying errands, and, with the marshal's daily accounting for the number of horses, shows the fluctuations in size of the countess's household.

A considerable number of visitors were listed – over fifty names are mentioned in the seven months of the account – and many of them were accompanied by large retinues. However, it should be remembered that everyone whose normal place was not in the countess's household was specified on the roll as an outsider. For example, when Earl Simon came with his own large army to spend the two weeks before Easter at Odiham, he was listed as a visitor; so, too, were the elder sons, on their occasional appearances to see their mother. Others who appear frequently are the senior officials of the household, whose business led them back and forth between the earl and the countess, wherever they might be, and also took them up and down to London for purchases.

The true guests were of many types: royal officials, knights of the shire who were staunch supporters of the earl, and men who had previously served as local officials for the earl and now had a share in the administration of the country. It is interesting to note that in a period which might reasonably seem to discourage unarmed travellers, the countess also entertained a large number of religious personages. Some were definitely friends of the Leicesters and supporters of the baronial cause, such as the abbot of

Waverley, the Cistercian abbey so close to Odiham. Others, such as the prioress of Wintney and the prioress of Amesbury, seem to have been trying to complete business for their convents.[1]

But nuns were not the only women travelling, either for business or for pleasure. Some of the greatest ladies of the realm were among the countess's visitors. Isabella de Fortibus, for example, spent the Easter weekend at Odiham, and the countess of Oxford visited in May. Her appearance is less surprising since her husband was a strong supporter of Earl Simon.

The titled and the wealthy are easily classifiable, but sometimes it is possible to trace the lines of self-interest and feudal relationship which lie behind the unexplained and unfamiliar names in the roll. Margery de Crek is a particularly good example of the many possible ties. Margery came to visit the countess at Odiham in March, travelling with a retinue of twelve horses.[2] She was almost certainly a widow. Her husband, Bartholomew de Crek, had been in Ireland in 1224 in the service of William Marshal, the Countess Eleanor's first husband, and in 1232, after the earl's death, was described as Eleanor's yeoman. By 1235 he had married Margery, held lands in Norfolk and Suffolk and, like many others richer than himself, was deeply in debt to some Jews of London. His upward social climb was ultimately crowned by knighthood. The date of Bartholomew's death is not ascertainable, though his name disappears from the records after 1251.[3] Margery, however, lived many years as a widow, dying in 1282 when she must have been at least in her sixties. By this time she had retired with a fairly large household to the Augustinian convent of Flixton. She was quite a wealthy woman, and her will disposed of many of her goods in favour of the Flixton community.[4] Her son John died seven years after his mother, still holding Creake in Norfolk of the earl marshal, and Combe in Suffolk of the king in chief.[5] The original connection of Margery and

Bartholomew de Crek with the countess of Leicester was undoubtedly due to Bartholomew's service of William Marshal, who may have rewarded him with his original landholding. In any case ancient acquaintance, and perhaps the hope of present favours, kept Margery in friendly touch with the Countess Eleanor in the troubled year of 1265. This one case, in which the connecting links are reasonably easy to uncover, illustrates very clearly the involved tangle of political self-interest, feudal relationships, and even natural human companionship which formed the fabric of thirteenth-century feudal society.

Apart from her overnight guests, the Countess Eleanor seems to have been well aware that hospitality could serve political ends. During her trip from Odiham to the greater safety of Dover she entertained the burgesses of Winchelsea as she passed through their town. Only three days after she arrived at Dover she invited the burgesses of Sandwich to dinner, and both groups of burgesses were again asked to dinner at Dover Castle in July.[1] The reason for these invitations is abundantly clear, as the support of the important townsmen of the Cinque Ports was essential for the baronial cause. It was imperative that Eleanor should keep them loyal to Earl Simon, for they could guard the coast against French invasion, and keep out mercenaries recruited for the king overseas.

Correspondence, as well as hospitality, was put to political uses. An analysis of the Countess Eleanor's correspondents shows very clearly the wide-ranging interests of a great magnate and his wife, though its unusual extent was influenced by their extraordinary situation. The frequent use of letters was nothing new, for in more peaceful years Eleanor and Simon had corresponded with Bishop Grosseteste and Brother Adam Marsh, who was a fluent, if enigmatic, letter-writer. In the spring and summer of 1265 an unusual number of messages went back and forth between husband and wife. These were undoubtedly accounted for by the exigencies of the political and military situation. Indeed the messengers who carried the letters were among the busiest members of the household. Besides her husband, the countess corresponded with Richard Gravesend, bishop of Lincoln and enthusiast for the baronial cause, Thomas Cantilupe, the baronial chancellor, and her officials and favourite merchants among many others. Nor was this activity limited only to England. Messengers went back and forth between England and Bigorre, where the earl still claimed the title of count, and Laura de Montfort, Earl Simon's niece, wrote from the family castle at Montfort-l'Amaury. The frequent entries on the account are sufficient to show that the countess was extremely active in many fields, and that constant communication was possible whenever political or personal needs required it.

After the earl's defeat and death at Evesham, the countess's role was even more important and demanding. The responsibility for salvaging any fragment of the Montfort fortunes was hers alone. The account shows how she armed her intercessors with letters for her unforgiving brother the king when he held his first parliament after his return to unfettered power; and how she also wrote, with greater success, to Richard of Cornwall to ensure his good will and promise of assistance.[1] Not only did she arrange the departure of her youngest son for Bigorre, she also seems to have succeeded in smuggling 11,000 marks out of England to France.[2] In a final agreement made at Dover with the Lord Edward, Eleanor ensured the return to grace and favour of most of her household, though she herself had to leave the kingdom.[3] All these various achievements illustrate the many facets of the countess's executive ability and capacity for planning.

The household account gives glimpses of a great lady's many activities. From its evidence it is easy to see that many, in fact most, of her occupations were not particularly domestic, or even feminine in the restricted sense. The primary duty of a great baron's wife was to produce the heir necessary to carry on the line, and then to serve as an active partner with her husband in the many enterprises of feudal life. She might even, when necessary, take sole charge. The purely domestic routine of the lady of the house in such a vast establishment was discharged by a well-planned and carefully detailed organization which was responsible for the smooth running of the domestic machinery.

3

The Organisation of the Household

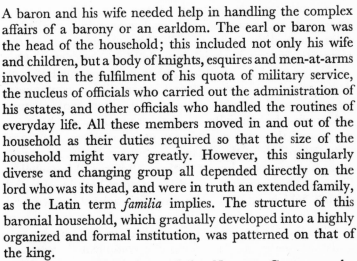

A baron and his wife needed help in handling the complex affairs of a barony or an earldom. The earl or baron was the head of the household; this included not only his wife and children, but a body of knights, esquires and men-at-arms involved in the fulfilment of his quota of military service, the nucleus of officials who carried out the administration of his estates, and other officials who handled the routines of everyday life. All these members moved in and out of the household as their duties required so that the size of the household might vary greatly. However, this singularly diverse and changing group all depended directly on the lord who was its head, and were in truth an extended family, as the Latin term *familia* implies. The structure of this baronial household, which gradually developed into a highly organized and formal institution, was patterned on that of the king.

Since the earliest days of the Norman Conquest, the barons of England had borrowed the king's administrative practices to help them in the task of running their own estates. At the same time they naturally copied the royal domestic organization, since there was no clear dividing line between private and public business. This tendency was encouraged by the many links which existed between the king and his barons. All the magnates were frequently with the king; consulting on matters of policy, seeking a favour or a grant, pursuing a lawsuit, or merely fulfilling their duty of attendance on the king's person on some ceremonial occasion. After all, the barons had a recognized share in the government of the realm, and they also had a practical knowledge of the operations of its various officials. Naturally the division of duties among their own officials, their accounting system, and the whole administrative plan of their own households, were copied from the royal pattern with which they were familiar. As the royal administrative system became more specialized and complex during the thirteenth century, the baronial households followed suit.

Although this development of the royal administrative system is well documented and has been carefully studied, it is far more difficult to describe the organization of the thirteenth-century baronial household in any detail. Our knowledge must be pieced together from fragmentary surviving records and the incidental information in contemporary treatises. The resultant picture is often contradictory and confused, especially as the terminology is still very vague, and the same official may exercise several functions.

By the middle of the thirteenth century, however, certain features seem to be characteristic of all baronial households. There was a seignorial council made up of both knights and officials which fulfilled the same function of advice and consent for its lord that the *curia regis* did for the king. There were auditors who normally travelled around the baron's lands, overseeing and checking the complicated system of accounts. Two officials dealt with financial matters, receiving income and making expenditures. Their titles varied on different estates, and they might be known a treasurer, receiver-general, or wardrober.* The keystone of the baronial household was the steward: he held courts, headed the lord's council, occasionally acted as an attorney at the king's

* The wardrobe was not only the name of a special room where valuables were kept, it also became the technical term for the king's or baron's private treasury. The "wardrober" was in charge of this wardrobe, or treasury, a function which had grown out of his original duties as keeper of the robes. A series of wardrobe accounts, which give the inflow of money, as well as the outgo itemized in the household account, became fairly general in the last quarter of the thirteenth century.

court, supervised, and often appointed, such local officials as bailiffs and reeves, and acted as his lord's deputy. These various officials were the important nucleus who carried on the day-to-day affairs of the barony. Their number and their exact function depended on the importance and wealth of the lord whom they served.

A list of officials for the barony of Eresby in the last quarter of the thirteenth century gives a good idea of the actual household of even a minor baron, and also suggests the large number of officials and servants concerned with purely domestic affairs. The lord of Eresby had a steward who was a knight, and a wardrober who was the chief clerical officer and examined the daily expenditures with the steward every night. The wardrober's deputy was clerk of the offices, and the chaplain and almoner could be required to help write letters and documents or act as controller of expenses. There were also two friars with their boy clerk who could substitute for the chaplain. The purely domestic officials and servants were numerous. They included a chief buyer, a marshal, two pantrymen and butlers, two cooks and larderers, a saucer – the medieval term for the sauce cook – and a poulterer, two ushers and chandlers, a porter, a baker, a brewer, and two farriers. These men were assisted by their own boy helpers.[1] This actual list has the great advantage of illustrating the dual character of the officials who made up the baron's household, and the number of individuals who travelled with it on its many moves. The most important officials were only incidentally concerned with daily affairs. They dealt primarily with the long-range problems of the administration of the scattered lands and the collection of the various revenues of the barony, serving as the overseers and directors of such rooted local officials as reeves, bailiffs, or constables. But the nucleus of officials also included those whose total concern was with the daily domestic routine, and one man above all – the steward of the household – was primarily responsible for the smooth running of daily life.

Although in the twelfth century one steward had supervised both the lord's estates and his household, by the mid-
thirteenth century there were normally two men both
known as stewards for these separate functions. The more
important was described simply as the steward, and was in
charge of the estates; the lesser, referred to as the steward
of the household, was in charge of the daily routine and the
domestic servants. The estates steward was often of noble
birth, only a little below the status of the lord he served, and
indeed his position was often a stepping-stone to wealth and
royal promotion. It is more difficult to define the social
position of the steward of the household, but there seems little
doubt that he was usually a man of lesser importance and
lower birth. His office appears to have been an end in itself
rather than an accepted rung on the ladder of advancement.

The distinction between the spheres of these two officials
is also emphasized by the two kinds of accounts which were
common in the administrative system of an earldom or
even a great barony. The estates steward and the auditors
were concerned with the annual accounts rendered by the
local officials for all the lands, fees, and miscellaneous
revenues of the earldom. These accounts listed the revenues,
acreage, produce, and livestock, as well as the necessary
expenses, on each of an earl's many manors, the scutages
and feudal aids from fees, as well as the many money rents
and the profits from courts. The Ministers' Accounts as they
were called, can provide a detailed picture of the many little
units that went to make up a great earldom. The accounts
for 1296–7 for the great earldom of Cornwall have been
published, and they show how nothing was too small for
the report of the bailiff and the vigilant eye of the auditor.
Thus the men who answer for the great castle of Wallingford
carefully include in their account the fact that there was no
increase in swans from one of the three nests, because the
eggs were carried away in the floods; and the steward of
Mere includes in his list of stores a pair of white gloves

rendered as rent at Michaelmas.[1] Ministers' Accounts specify the individual sources of income.

The household account, on the other hand, detailed minutely the way in which the lord's money was disbursed. It was the particular responsibility of the steward of the household and was drawn up each night under his immediate supervision. Within the limits of its own prescribed form the household account holds a mirror to everyday life. One of the more endearing habits of the medieval scribe when dealing with accounts was his tendency to particularize every tiny item. He had no column headed 'miscellaneous expenses', and the minuteness of the record helps to give more of the flavour of the time. Even the specimen accounts include such homely touches as the expenses for mending the sheets and buying the mustard.[2]

In a very great household it was not unusual to have two household accounts; one for the earl and one for the countess. This imitated the royal practice of having separate households for the king, the queen, and the royal children, each of which had its own set of officials and accounts. The account of Henry, King Edward's small son who died in 1274 at the age of five, describes a household made up of Henry and his sister and their cousin John of Brittany, their nurses, officials, and servants, who lived quite apart from the royal household.[3] The earl and countess of Leicester had such a divided system, at least in 1265. The earl's household was, of course, the dominant one. When Earl Simon and his enormous retinue came to Odiham before Easter, only their expenses for the first day were charged on the countess's roll; all the costs for the following two weeks were charged to the earl[4] and presumably listed in detail on his household account.

As the children of an earl or great baron grew up and had a retinue of their own with which they travelled separately from their parent's household, they too kept account of their daily expenses in a household account. The roll of expenses of John of Brabant, son-in-law of Edward I, covers only that young man's personal expenditures and has a distinctly jaunty air, since it is filled with items about falcons, horses, games, fine clothes, and minstrels.[1] John and his travelling companions, Henry and Thomas of Lancaster, were not weighed down by the need to provide food, drink, and the other necessities of life for a large establishment. Roger Leyburn, the able general and companion of the Lord Edward, was given the task of campaigning against the baronial rebels in Essex, the Weald and the Cinque Ports after Evesham; included with his statement of expenses for his military services to the king is a day-to-day account of his kitchen and stable expenses, written in the accepted form of the household roll.[2]

All the evidence shows that the keeping of household rolls was the normal practice of the upper classes. It is only because so few have survived for the thirteenth century that we tend to overlook this fact. Two of the most complete thirteenth-century household rolls deal with clerical households: that of Richard Swinfield, bishop of Hereford, for 1289–90,[3] and the wardrobe and household account of Bogo de Clare, brother of the earl of Gloucester, for 1284–6.[4] These households, though clerical, were of baronial standing and shared many common features with the system of private administration and the routine of daily life natural to the lay magnates.

The countess of Leicester's roll follows the general pattern. Normally a roll covered a full year, running from Michaelmas to Michaelmas. However the Countess Eleanor's account is fragmentary, and the thirteen surviving membranes deal only with the days between February 19th and August 29th. There is no daily accounting for the expenses of September, though some of the miscellaneous expenses of that month have been listed. On the face of each membrane the expenses for each day are described separately. These always included, and in the same order, the amount or cost of grain or bread, the wine and beer, the supplies for the kitchen, and the supplies for the stable. The number of horses was carefully listed, and the amount of hay and oats provided were credited to the account of the reeve of the manor which furnished them. A sum was made up for the expenses of each day and, when the end of a membrane was reached, a sum was then made for the whole of that membrane. No specific number of days were allotted to each membrane, and it varied in practice. The amounts paid over to the countess's officials who bought spices on her behalf were also listed on the face of the membrane, as well as various occasional payments; but in general the incidental matters were given on the back of each membrane where all kinds of unrelated items, of about the same period as the detailed daily accounting on the front, were listed. Sometimes a sum was made on the back, sometimes not.

A late thirteenth-century treatise known as *Fleta** has a valuable section on how the household account was drawn up, and specifies precisely the various functions of the household steward:

It is the steward's duty to account every night in person or through a deputy (appointed, however, by the lord) with the buyer, marshal, cook, spencer, and other officials, for the expenses of the household, and to ascertain the total of the day's expenditures. It is his duty also to take delivery by tally from the larder, at the hands of the reeve, of flesh and fish of every kind as may be necessary, and this he shall have cut up into portions in his presence and counted as they are delivered to the cook and for these he shall hear a reasonable account. It is also his business to know precisely how many farthing loaves can be made from a quarter of wheat, and the pantler

* *Fleta* was primarily a lawbook, compiled c. 1290, which drew heavily on Glanvill and Bracton. Its discussion of private administration and the duties and requirements of various officers of the king's court is mainly original and shows that the author had an intimate and personal knowledge of these particular matters.

is bound to receive this number from the baker. Further he should know how many loaves and how many portions are appropriate for the normal household on ordinary days. . . . And all the serjeants are answerable, jointly and severally, to the steward for their offices. And he is bound to bear witness to what they do.[1]

The steward of the household was obviously a fully occupied man of some education and training.

Already, by the mid-thirteenth century, energetic teachers were providing the necessary training for such officials. It is amusing to discover business administration established as a quasi-academic subject so long ago. From the time of Henry III there existed at Oxford certain teachers who specialized in the "useful" subjects. These included writing, Latin composition, French, the drafting of charters, the keeping of accounts, and even the holding of courts. The teachers were not members of the university, though they worked in a university town and drew many of their students from those who had been deflected from the long struggle for a degree. The instruction given was strictly practical, for its function was to lay the necessary theoretical foundation for the many-sided work of a man of affairs. These early teachers have come to light through their treatises on conveyancing, letter-writing, accounting, and legal procedure, produced as models for their pupils. To make their model letters more realistic, they frequently discussed a common situation with contemporary references, and so revealed their own practice. From such allusions it appears that it took about six months or a year to learn the work of an official. This short period was often chosen by those who discovered that their bent was not academic, and who had also been fortunate enough to receive the favourable notice of some lord who was willing to use them as officials.[2] After this brief academic introduction the new official must have had to learn the rest of his duties by harsh practical experience.

However trained, the steward was often the butt of the

story-teller and the moralist. The ridiculous Malvolio was after all the steward of Olivia's household; and poking fun at the steward was a recognized literary convention long before Shakespeare. The steward's position made him subject to many temptations which, to judge from the literature of the period, he did not resist very strenuously. Naturally any story which ended with the discomfiture of a powerful official was perpetually popular with the lower classes, since they were convinced that he feathered his own nest at their expense. A typical contemporary story, and less scurrilous than most, is a French tale, *Le Dit du Buffet*, in which a poverty-stricken cowherd humiliated a rich and greedy steward. This official had grown fat as a pig at his master's expense and had compounded his unpopularity by being overbearing and mean to those below him. The steward's lord had invited everyone to a free feast, and the cowherd, though dirty and unkempt, decided to try his luck at enjoying this liberality. The peasant succeeded in entering the hall, though the steward gave him a buffet on the ear for his presumption, but he could find no place on the benches. The steward gave him a small cushion – also known as a buffet – to sit on, but warned him that it was only a loan and must be given back afterwards. After the feast the count offered a robe of new scarlet to the man who could make the company laugh the loudest. The minstrels and jugglers played the fool, sang, fiddled, and told risqué stories in their efforts to win the prize. Finally the cowherd came forward and, with his work-hardened hand, gave the steward a terrific buffet on the ear, reminding him of the loan, and remarking that it was wrong not to to repay what one had been lent. He added that he would even pay it back with interest if so required. Laughing at the steward's confusion, the company awarded the quick-witted cowherd the robe of scarlet.[1]

It is hard to know whether a large proportion of stewards were as rich or as greedy as the one described in this tale, but it was certainly a common problem. The New Testament parable of the unjust steward suggests that the difficulty was not new, and could take many forms. Few officials can have been as ingenious in their cupidity as the bailiff mentioned by Jacques de Vitry*in one of his sermons, who persuaded his lord to sell the sunshine, by charging 12d for each cloth that was laid out to bleach or dry in the sun.[1] Robert Mannyng†, in his penitential manual, vigorously denounced all such counsellors and stewards who made life impossible for the poor man by their harsh enforcement of wicked laws. With uncompromising zest, Robert condemned them all – lords, stewards, and counsellors together – to "Go to hell, both top and tayle".[2]

Apart from the household steward who is not identified, the household roll of the countess of Leicester gives the names and functions of many of the lesser officials and servants. In a large household like hers, which included over sixty servants, one of the most acute problems must have been the choice of efficient staff. The standard set by the didactic writers was exceedingly high. Jacques de Vitry insisted that the good servant must not only have a clean mouth, clean hands and a clean mind, but he could not be either a liar, a slanderer a flatterer, a babbler, or even too, talkative.[3] Grosseteste's *Rules* also laid down most emphatically the kind of behaviour required from the members of the household on pain of dismissal. It was his ideal that "no one is to be kept in your household if you have not reasonable

* Jacques de Vitry was the best-known French preacher of the first half of the thirteenth century. He preached the Albigensian Crusade, was elected Bishop of Acre in 1216, and spent more than ten years in the Holy Land and the Latin kingdoms of the east. After this he returned to France and continued preaching.

† Robert Mannyng of Brunne, or Bourne in southern Lincolnshire, was a priest and, for a time, a Gilbertine canon. He translated the thirteenth-century *Manuel des Pechiez* by William of Waddington into English, and added considerable material. Robert's version is entitled *Handlyng Synne*, and was written at the beginning of the fourteenth century.

belief that they are faithful, discreet, painstaking and honest, and of good manners". It seems sadly obvious that the ideal was infrequently realized for the bishop went on to say that "if they are disloyal, unwise, filthy in person, unprofitable, gluttonous, quarrelsome or drunken", they should be turned out.[1] Deploring servants' deficiencies has been a fruitful topic for many centuries, and the thirteenth was no exception.

Occasionally it is possible to identify more fully the officials named briefly in the countess's account. Richard of Havering, for example, had served the earl of Leicester as steward since 1251,[2] and held one-fourth of a knight's fee from him. He also had other lands and rents, including one parcel for which the annual rent was one rose rendered to the landlord.[3] His social background and landholdings suggest the typical estates steward – a knight of moderate wealth and social position. He was trusted by the earl with the custody of Wallingford castle in the summer of 1265, but after Evesham was pardoned by Edward and the king.[4] William of Wortham was, from the evidence of the account, a trusted official of the countess of Leicester, making many of her major purchases. He too had been closely associated with the Montforts for some years, and perhaps had come to the earl from the household of Bishop Grosseteste.[5] William joined Earl Simon's army, accompanied him to that last desperate struggle in the west, and fell beside him at Evesham.[6]

While we can uncover the occasional incident in the careers of some of the more important officials who served the earl and countess of Leicester, it is difficult to describe their functions in the household with any great degree of accuracy, or to see clearly the skeleton of the administrative system. The Ministers' Accounts would be more precise, but none have been discovered for the Leicester earldom in this period. On the other hand the roll itself shows that the organization of the household in the mid-thirteenth century was still sufficiently fluid to allow duties to be interchanged on occasion, so that any of these officials might undertake a number of tasks. Such an interchange would be particularly likely at the time of the countess's roll, covering as it does the most crucial period of baronial government and final defeat. Many of the normal conventions might well have been bypassed in the increasing demand for loyal fighting men and the stress of preparation for battle, so that even the usual lines are less clearly drawn.

Apart from the senior officials, there was another group which was essential to the maintenance of the household organization. These were the chaplains and the clerks. If the countess followed the example of her brother the king, she used one of her chaplains to take charge of her offerings to the poor. The office of royal almoner was an exacting one. According to *Fleta*:

> He is to gather up the fragments diligently every day and distribute them to the needy; he is to visit for charity's sake the sick, the lepers, the captive, the poor, the widows and others in want and the wanderers in the countryside, and to receive cast horses, clothing, money, and other gifts, bestowed in alms and to distribute them faithfully. He ought also by frequent exhortations to spur the king to liberal almsgiving, especially on Saints' Days, and to implore him not to bestow his robes, which are of great price, upon players, flatterers, fawners, talebearers, or minstrels, but to command them to be used to augment his almsgiving.[1]

The countess's almoner would have had less scope, but the same sort of duties, though he was not much plagued by minstrels. In fact, the countess fulfilled her charitable duties with considerable generosity. John Scot, who was in charge of her offerings throughout the roll, was provided with an average of 4d a day for the poor. This was in addition to food – both the usual fragments, and the occasional special dinner. In comparison, Bogo de Clare, the rich and pluralist cleric who was the brother of the earl of Gloucester, was extremely niggardly in his alms. Even on a great feast day, when the rest of the expenses of his household were very high, he offered only 1d.[1]

The problem of finding a satisfactory chaplain for the household seems to have concerned the earl and countess for many years. When their friend Adam Marsh, the great Franciscan, was alive they corresponded with him about the matter. Adam was worried about the type of cleric to be introduced into the household. The friar insisted that he must "be devoted to the divine sacraments, strenuous in the ecclesiastical offices, honest in manners, and circumspect in actions". He added ruefully that the church is lacking in such men.[2] Finally Adam Marsh succeeded in sending to the earl and countess when they were in Gascony one of the most eminent of the contemporary Franciscans, Brother Gregory de Bosellis. This friar was in such demand that the earl and countess do not seem to have been able to keep him with them very long, for he later accompanied the archbishop of Canterbury to the papal court. It is possible that their friendship with Brother Gregory may even have antedated their acquaintance with Adam Marsh, for Gregory was the first lecturer to the friars at Leicester, probably around 1240.[3] Simon de Montfort had a well-earned reputation for generosity to the friars near his lands, and was on very good terms with them. Indeed in later years the earl had no more enthusiastic supporters than the friars, who praised in fulsome terms his sanctity and devotion to the offices of the church.

Friar or secular, a chaplain was a necessity. Once when the earl was in need of a chaplain in Gascony he simply walked off with the vicar of Salisbury, who was already charged with the cure of souls at the church of Odiham. Adam Marsh was shocked by Earl Simon's high-handed action and wrote to him in the most vigorous terms, charging him to send back the vicar "as shepherd to his own sheep . . . for the honour of God, for your salvation, for the need of the church".[4] Unfortunately, the earl's answer to this

E   65

impassioned plea has not come to light, but, despite the rebuke, the fondness of the earl and countess for Adam Marsh remained unabated.

One of the chaplain's assistants – Guillot in the countess's account – served as clerk of the chapel. The safe-keeping and the supervision of the packing and transport of the vestments, vessels, and other necessities for mass were his particular duty, and frequently one sumpter-horse was set aside to carry this chapel furniture. Among the items for which the clerk of the chapel was responsible might be a portable altar, such as that allowed to the earl of Pembroke in 1290 by special papal licence. This permitted his chaplain to say mass for the household at any convenient spot.[1] Portable altars had a long history, for they were mentioned by the Venerable Bede. Normally they were rectangular slabs about twenty inches long, with a centre of marble or other fine stone covering a relic and framed in a thick panel of rare wood. This frame was often decorated with engraved or enamelled plates of metal and adorned with precious stones.[2] Bishop Swinfield's account also mentions four wooden candlesticks, which may equally have been meant for his journeys.[3]

Besides the official chaplain, almoner, and clerk of the chapel, there were other clerks who wrote letters and kept accounts under the supervision of the higher officials. They must have been especially busy in the countess's household in 1265 for, as has already been mentioned, Eleanor's range of correspondence was particularly wide that spring and summer. Some of the clerks appear as individuals with special duties. Christopher and Eudes were the clerks who wrote the roll, and each of them inserted a marginal note where he took up the task, although it is obvious that Eudes' handwriting is a good deal neater and more legible than that of Christopher. From the evidence of the account, Walter appears to have been the most important of the clerks, and to have served primarily as clerk of the offices, with considerable authority. He frequently went to London on errands, and often supervised the purchases of cloth made by the tailor as well as the buying of necessary spices. After the household had moved to Dover Walter was constantly charged with the buying of oats for the horses, as the ordinary system of supply from the manors had broken down under the unusual conditions of that summer.

The chaplains and clerks were minor officials of the household; beneath them functioned a hierarchy of domestic servants. The recognized division of these servants and their various duties are emphasized in a legal settlement made between the abbot of Westminster and one of his tenants in 1215. The abbot, like a bishop, was the head of a great household, perhaps even more carefully organized than that of a secular baron, and just as peripatetic. One of the perennial points of dispute between these great churchmen and their tenants was to what degree the abbot must be given hospitality – and for how long, as this could be a very expensive matter. According to this particular settlement seven of the abbot's servants were to precede him at his tenant's manor. They were to be given charge of the seven departments of the house: the seneschal was to have charge of the hall, the chamberlain of the chamber, the butler of the buttery and the drink, the usher of the door, the cook of the kitchen, and the marshal of the marshalsea.[1] Even this early in the century, the sharp distinction of functions is obvious, as well as the existence of a carefully thought out organization. Some of these upper servants must have been the necessary advance party to any move of a large household. Thus when the earl of Gloucester was on his way to York for the marriage of King Henry's daughter in 1251, he sent Richard his master cook, William his marshal, and Walter the clerk of his chamber ahead of him to secure lodgings at Stamford. Since the servants were also leading three greyhounds, they were tempted to take a doe in the royal forest and fell foul of the royal foresters.[2]

The countess of Leicester's account mentions Simon the cook, Andrew the butler, and Ralph the baker, as well as their various helpers. Curiosity is particularly aroused by one kitchen helper called "Garbag". There were also two lads of the chamber and several tailors, of whom Hicque was apparently the chief. Apart from the nurses, who were of rather higher social standing, the only feminine domestic servant named was the laundress, who was an indispensable adjunct to any household. She was, however, one of the poorest paid of the servants, as the average rate seems to have been only 1d a day.[1] The laundress's hard work was a favourite topic of medieval sermons, which even went into considerable detail about her use of lye and how it was made. The preachers described vividly how she had to turn and beat and wash and hang to get the clothes clean.[2] The yearly wages of Petronilla, the countess of Leicester's laundress, do not appear in the roll, though she did receive her shoes for the Easter term (worth 12d) as well as an additional payment of 15d on May 31st for the laundry from Christmas.[3] There is no mention of any laundress at Dover, so perhaps Petronilla remained at Odiham. A laundress might be asked to do more than wash clothes. Indeed, the hangers-on of the military camps were usually described as washer-women, though they practised an even older profession. In Bogo de Clare's account a specific payment was made each week to the laundress for washing the lord's head,[4] a surprisingly personal duty.

Certain individuals mentioned in the Montfort account had a particularly close relationship with either the earl or the countess. For example, the countess's damsels were not servants, but rather companions of lower social standing. Another personal attendant was the barber. Probably he was the earl's personal servant who returned to the countess after his master's death. In any case he had not been with the countess's household long enough to perform his other function as surgeon and blood-letter. During the winter

68

Eleanor had had to send to Reading for a barber, and had even rented a horse to get him to Odiham to bleed one of the damsels.[1]

The most important of the outside servants was the marshal, who was in charge of the horses and the needs of the stable. Under his orders there was the smith, or farrier, whose work in keeping the horses shod and the irons of the carts mended was a vital factor in maintaining the mobility of the household. The carters were another large group responsible for the transport of goods. They were constantly busy in a household as big as that of the countess of Leicester, and of course were in particular demand at the time when the household goods, as well as its members, had to be moved cross-country to Dover. Messengers were also much in evidence in the account, and their names suggest that they were specially chosen for their duties. Slingawai, Gobithesti, Trubodi, and Picard appear frequently in the account because their expenses were paid before they were dispatched; they could also expect to receive presents or money when they delivered their message. The countess's messengers were not among her higher-ranking servants, but they were most useful members of the household in the conditions of 1265.

At the base of this hierarchical pyramid of domestic servants, both indoors and out, were the great mass of anonymous grooms and boy attendants. They included huntsmen, as well as the lads who minded the horses and the hounds, or served as helpers and scullions for the upper servants. Their wages were low, and they were often recruited locally. When the household moved on these casual servants were paid off and dismissed.

Two outstanding impressions emerge from a rapid survey of the thirteenth-century household as illustrated by the Countess Eleanor's account: one is of the large, and variable number of people who made up such a household; the other is the flexibility of the organization which dealt with them.

Despite the constant change in personnel – servants are mentioned and then disappear from view – there continued to be a solid nucleus. This core of officials who travelled consistently with the earl and countess could carry on, in an undisturbed and relatively efficient fashion, the pattern of everyday life wherever the household might find itself.

4

The Daily Fare

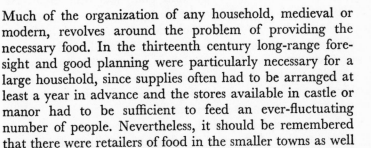

Much of the organization of any household, medieval or modern, revolves around the problem of providing the necessary food. In the thirteenth century long-range foresight and good planning were particularly necessary for a large household, since supplies often had to be arranged at least a year in advance and the stores available in castle or manor had to be sufficient to feed an ever-fluctuating number of people. Nevertheless, it should be remembered that there were retailers of food in the smaller towns as well as the larger cities. Besides butchers, bakers, brewers, and fishmongers, other tradesmen sold cooked foods. The familiar piemaker sold pasties of meat or fish, hot and well-peppered; other men peddled such delicacies as flawns, a kind of custard or cheese-cake, and wafers, the thin biscuits cooked in wafer-irons. All these trades were carefully described in contemporary lists of occupations.[1]

Although it was usual for large households on the move to carry their own supplies, it was possible for even a great number of people to buy a whole meal when travelling. When the countess of Leicester moved her household from Odiham to Dover, she stopped for dinner on the road at Chichester, Battle, and Romney. The cost of the whole meal varied astonishingly for no apparent reason, from 14d to 27s 5½d.[2] However these were extraordinary occasions. When a baronial household was in residence in one of its castles it was supplied from the stores already laid up within that castle, or brought from one of the lord's nearby manors. These local provisions were then supplemented by any necessary purchases. The Countess Eleanor's roll reflects the upheaval in the realm by its abnormal dependence on out-side purchases at the end of the summer, as the manorial economy buckled under the weight of civil war; in this way it is not altogether a faithful reflection of the normal practices of a great establishment.

The necessary foods were few in number, but the difference in diet between rich and poor was very great. All classes relied on bread as the daily mainstay, but the poor might be unable to add much more to their dark loaf than onions and coarse greens, with the occasional luxury of pork or a scrawny hen for special feasts. Any extra meat which could be taken from the fields or woods was a welcome luxury, though poaching of game reserved for the king or some great baron was a serious offence.

The baronial household, however, could choose from a fairly long list of commodities. Bread was still the basis of all meals, but it was closely followed by meat or fish, depending on whether the day was or was not one of fast. Eggs were generally used in large quantities, as was poultry, but on the whole as ingredients in other dishes; they were not eaten on their own. Fruits and vegetables are among the hardest things to trace because they were so rarely purchased. Anything which came directly from the castle garden or orchard was used in the kitchen without mention on the account, since it was neither paid for nor listed in the stores. Cheese, butter and milk appear occasionally in the accounts, though not frequently enough to make it possible to judge whether the countess had her own dairy-maid at Odiham. All these items, except the bread, were listed on the day's account under the heading of supplies for the kitchen, and the cook not only had to busy himself with the preparation of the dishes, he also had to render account to the steward each evening for every course at table.[1]

Bread was listed separately on the account, as befitted its central place in the diet. In any good-sized household, even one much smaller than that of the countess of Leicester, there was a baker who was an indispensable member of the establishment. One of the clerks was frequently entrusted with the particular task of supervising the amount of grain and flour given to the baker. This same clerk had to ensure that the proper number of loaves were delivered to the keeping of the pantler after the baking. However, the baker had a few recognized perquisites. According to the Assize of Bread, which attempted to regulate the standards and price of bread all over England, the baker should have a profit of 4d and the bran for each quarter of wheat, and two loaves for the baking fee. As legitimate expenses he could claim 1½d for three servants, ½d for two boys, ½d for yeast, 2d for wood, 1½d for bolting-cloths, and even a farthing for the candle. He was supposed to sell 418 pounds of bread from every quarter, and anything above that amount was vantage bread for himself.[1]

The references to bread in the accounts are confusing to translate. Although the Latin word is always *panis* the context makes it obvious that this must usually be translated as grain, since the amounts are given in quarters or bushels. A quarter officially contained eight bushels, but its actual size often varied, depending on whether it was heaped or "striked", that is levelled off. Indeed, the whole system of medieval measures is so bewildering that one of the more recent students of the subject has written in despair: "For medieval England one is left with little more than a legendary Winchester bushel, a linguistic red herring, and thirty-two grains of wheat."[2]

Equally confusing are the many different estimates as to the number of loaves to be expected from the somewhat uncertain unit of the quarter. One of the best modern authorities suggests that the quarter of grain should provide from 350 to 500 pounds of flour, and that a pound of flour should make a pound of bread.[3] The Assize of Bread tried to solve these problems by laying down standards for the proper weight of the various kinds of bread. It set a sliding scale by which all loaves were bought at a farthing, but their weight varied according to the price per quarter of wheat and the relative fineness of the bread. Six kinds were specifically – but not very clearly – described. Wastel was the finest white bread. The simnel, in those days, seems to have been a kind of biscuit, as it was defined as having been baked twice. The cocket loaf came in two varieties: the small cocket was of the same quality of flour as the wastel, but the large cocket was made of less expensive wheat. Whole-wheat bread appears to have been the kind in most common use, while treet bread was made of unbolted meal. The poorest of all was what was described as common wheat. It was very coarse, probably made chiefly of refuse stuff, and a farthing loaf of it weighed as much as two cocket loaves.[1] This description is admirably detailed, but does little to dispel our confusion, because other contemporary writers rarely use the terms of the assize. Bishop Grosseteste, for example, had a fixed standard for the number of loaves to be made from a quarter of wheat. He ordained that each quarter should provide 180 loaves, counting white and brown together,[2] although we may suspect that the finer breads came in smaller loaves than the coarser ones.

The immediate household of the countess of Leicester normally used five to six bushels of grain a day, but when the earl returned home with his large retinue the amount consumed climbed to forty-four bushels.[3] Most of her requirements were obtained from local manors: when the household was at Odiham, it was supplied from the earl's manor at Chalton; and at Dover, from the countess's manor of Brabourne. Private stocks, however, became depleted in the weeks before the harvest and were insufficient for the extra demands made upon them, so more and more had to be bought from the local merchants. The price paid for grain in any one year reflected in its wide variations the conditions of trade, the effect of weather on the harvest, and even the state of the realm. In the early '60s the price of a quarter of grain fluctuated between 3s 8d and 8s, while in 1265 the countess paid from 4s 4d to 5s.

Although the roll is reasonably informative about the price of grain, it is much less so about the types of bread which were made from it. An occasional entry suggests some differentiation between the bread used for the countess and that used for the kitchen, but it is not clear what this was. One striking feature is the amount of bread given to the dogs, the greyhounds of the countess and the hunting dogs of Henry and Guy de Montfort and Henry of Almain, which were kept at Odiham. On May 5th, the account mentions that bread for the dogs for ten days took three quarters of grain; but to feed the poor, over an eight-day period, took only half a quarter, though with the addition of thirteen gallons of beer.[1] An elusive term, *panis de froille*, is often used to describe the grain for the household. The earliest editor of the roll suggested that this meant ground corn,[2] but in any case it certainly refers to some process such as grinding or hulling, as there is also reference to oats *de froille*.

The countess's roll has no formal list of wages for the minor servants as does that of Bishop Swinfield. In his account a long list of winter and summer wages for the lesser officials and the servants is included on the back of the membranes; in the countess's account the money paid out in wages is entered indiscriminately with all the other miscellaneous expenditures. Roger, the bishop's baker, was paid 2s twice a year, while the boy attendant in the bakery received 3s for the whole year.[3] This is comparable with the wages paid Hande, the boy attendant in the countess's bakery, who received 7s for two years.[4] Baking apparently became more difficult when the countess's household moved to Dover and the facilities appear to have broken down, for another oven had to be built. It cost 6s 6d for the two masons and their servants, who took nine days in August to build it.[5] By baking their own requirements the countess's

household would not be troubled by the complicated provisions of the Assize of Bread, nor fleeced by those iniquitous
bakers described by the preachers. These rogues flooded their
dough with so much yeast that their deluded customers
might think they had bought bread, but in truth had only
purchased air.[1]

As important as bread in a wealthy household was the
other main element of medieval diet, meat or fish. The
standard flesh meats – beef, mutton, pork, and veal – were
varied by large amounts of poultry and eggs and, for the
privileged, by the venison brought in by the huntsmen.
Venison was a luxury, and one of the signs of post-Lenten
relaxation was the appearance of roebucks from the castle
stores and the manor among the meats given to the cook.[2]
At Dover venison was particularly welcome, since by the
end of August the countess's manors were no longer able to
provision the castle. Summer was the season for hunting the
buck and the hart, so this supply was probably fresh; but
the venison at Odiham was probably salted in the way that
the king's huntsmen salted the venison taken in the royal
forests before they sent it on to the king.

The price of the staple meats is rarely listed in the household accounts. In most cases the animals came from a
neighbouring manor and thus were credited to the reeve's
account. At other times a lump sum is given for several
different kinds of animals purchased at one time. Nevertheless, the Liberate Rolls provide a convenient contemporary
price list since they specify the amounts paid for the meats
brought to London for the celebration of the feast of St
Edward on January 5th, 1265. At this time oxen were
purchased for the king at 9s each, fresh pigs at 3s 6d, hams
at 16d, and sheep at 12d. As a particularly festive touch there
were also ten boars, at a cost of 9s 7d each.[3]

All these meats were either salted for convenient storage,
or kept alive near the kitchen till the cook required them.
Poultry was always fresh and was used in enormous quanti-

ties. The various kinds are not always differentiated, but the countess's account does specify geese and capons as well as the ordinary fowl. Capons were always more expensive than other poultry because they were properly fattened in coops on oats. Nothing, however, was allowed to go to waste from this investment in their feeding, for their grease was used as a lubricant for cart wheels and for sheep-dressing.[1] Thus a capon cost between 2 and 3d, while the ordinary hen might be bought for as little as ½d and rarely cost more than a penny. Geese, too, cost between 2d and 3d, and were a little more highly thought of than the common hen. None of the really exotic birds, such as peacocks and cranes, which frequently graced the royal table, appeared on the countess's account; but Roger Leyburn's account mentions six peacocks presented to him as a gift – probably from someone who considered it wise to propitiate the king's representative with such a valuable present.[2]

Beef and mutton appeared almost invariably upon the menu on any non-fast day. Many of the members of a household like that of the Leicesters might well echo the complaint which served as an exercise in grammar some two centuries later: "I have no delyte in beffe and motyn and such daily metes. I wolde onys have a partrige set before us, or sum other such, and in especiall litell small birdes that I love passyngly well."[3] Partridge in the thirteenth century seems to have been a rare and special treat. Two partridges were bought for Henry and his sister Eleanor, the children of Edward I, on one occasion, but they cost 4½d, a large sum for such small birds.[4]

Good agricultural practice required the total use of all the by-products of cows and sheep, as well as their flesh and hides. Such practical treatises as that by Walter of Henley*

---

* Walter of Henley was the thirteenth-century author of an enormously popular treatise on agriculture, known as *Walter of Henley's Husbandry*. This treatise continued in practical use for several centuries, but the career and background of the author are still disputed.

defined the amount of butter and cheese which could normally be expected from cows and ewes under different conditions of pasturage. Sometimes grasping landlords could carry economy too far, for it seems to have been a common practice to kill sick sheep, have their meat salted and dried, and then distribute it to the servants and labourers in the household. Walter of Henley thought this was carrying thrift altogether too far and vigorously denounced the practice.[1] Such use of rotten meat and fish by merchants and innkeepers was frequent enough to bring down the strongest denunciations of the preachers. Jacques de Vitry summed up the prevalent situation when he told of a seller of cooked meat whose customer boasted of having bought meat from no one else for seven years. The astounded butcher replied: "You have done this for so long a time and you still live?"[2]

Despite the large amounts of meat, fish played an even more dominant part in the account. This is partly because the roll covers the Lenten period, and also because Wednesday, Friday, and Saturday were usually fish days all the year round. Then, whenever friars were visitors at dinner fish had to be provided for them, as they were forbidden meat. The accounts from Odiham and Dover show the great difference between the fish available inland and the more interesting varieties which abounded at the Channel ports. For all medieval households anywhere, the humble salted herring was the staple of the menu on fish days, and only cost about 10d the hundred*. Yarmouth was the great centre of herring fishing, and its red or white herring – depending on whether they were smoked or salted – were prized all over England. Fresh herring were a particular delicacy, even for the king. The city of Norwich had to render annually to the king twenty-four pies of the first fresh herring. There was to be no skimping either, on the contents of the pies, for each one had to contain five herrings

* Herring was usually reckoned by the long hundred of six score, which was the normal measure for fish in the Middle Ages.

and be flavoured with ginger, pepper, cinnamon, and other spices. Carrying these pies safely to the king was the rent for a tract of land near Norwich, and the courtier was to be rewarded with a pie as well as a liberal allowance of food and drink when he arrived at court.[1] The royal pies were a luxury, but there was nothing luxurious about the average herring. Most people had it salted and by the end of Lent were desperately tired of it:

> Thou wyll not beleve how wery I am off fyshe, and how moch I desir that flesh wer cum in ageyn, for I have ate non other but salt fysh this Lent, and it hath engendyrde so moch flewme within me that it stoppith my pyps that I can unneth speke nother brethe.[2]

The plaint of the fifteenth-century schoolboy struck a very common chord. Since the countess of Leicester's household consumed from four hundred to a thousand herrings a day during Lent, it is easy to understand how attractive the more liberal diet of the Easter season seemed.

Apart from herring, many other varieties of fish were eaten, and some unusual ones were thought a luxury in the thirteenth century. Whale, sturgeon and porpoise were highly regarded. Both the whale and the sturgeon were royal fish, and the author of *Fleta* insisted that it was the royal privilege to have all of the sturgeon, but it was sufficient if the king had the head of the whale and the queen the tail.[3] Whale appeared on the countess of Leicester's roll, listed among the spices. Two hundred (either weight or pieces, the roll does not say which) cost 34s, and an amount worth 6s 1d was left at Kenilworth for the use of the countess's brother, Richard of Cornwall. A barrel of sturgeon, worth 31s, was also left at Kenilworth for him when the rest of the spices were brought on to Odiham for the Leicester household.[4]

During the household's residence at Odiham there is little description of the types of fish eaten. There is the occasional reference to mackerel and to stockfish, another common dried and smoked fish. Generally the clerk merely lists "fish" at a certain price. Whatever the types bought, the ordinary supplies for the household were either insufficient or unsatisfactory when Earl Simon came to Odiham during Lent. Simon the Fisherman, who was a permanent member of the household on yearly wages, was sent off to nearby Farnham with some helpers to catch fish for the earl in the fishponds of the bishop of Winchester.[1]

Fishponds were a valuable adjunct to any manor, as both Odiham and Manorbier bear witness, and a conscientious lord would often build one to enhance his property. Richard of Cornwall, for example, improved his manor of Isleworth by building a fine fishpond there, though it was temporarily destroyed by the unruly London adherents of the baronial party who sacked the manor.[2] These fishponds were usually dug out in a rectangular shape, near a spring or perhaps a small stream. Banked earth was used to provide a moderate depth in the pool while allowing a gentle flow of water through it. Occasionally there would be an elaborate chain of pools, with different chambers for different kinds of fish, and perhaps even places for breeding.[3] The medieval fishpond was a most ingenious construction, carefully designed to take the best possible advantage of nature.

Although the countess of Leicester fed her own household rather frugally, luxuries appeared when special guests were entertained. When the Lord Edward and Henry de Montfort came to Odiham in March the countess added sea fish, pike, and eels to the inevitable herring.[4] A big pike was considered a special treat, and it was one of the niceties of medieval etiquette that the biggest fish was served to the most honoured personage. Bishop Grosseteste once startled the earl of Gloucester by reprimanding the episcopal servants for serving the earl with a small fish while they gave the bishop a larger one. The earl was much surprised to find the bishop, whom he knew was of low birth, so well versed in the proper courtesies.[5] Pike were expensive; by the end of the thirteenth century a three-foot pike brought 6s 8d in London, the price of two pigs.[1] Obviously the countess made a special effort for the last day of the earl's visit to Odiham, as the account records oysters and lampreys.[2] Lampreys were a special favourite of King Henry. The best English ones came from the Severn, and early in his reign the king sent a rather pathetic order to the sheriff of Gloucester to send as many lampreys as he could acquire by purchase and otherwise, as all other fish but lampreys seemed insipid.[3] The conveyance of oysters to Odiham must have presented difficulties, but Roger Leyburn's account also mentions oysters, specifically described as raw. His were probably fresh, since he was on the Channel coast at the time.[4]

This problem of transport and preservation always bedevilled the inland dweller when buying fish. Of course the staples, herring, stockfish and cod, were normally sold salted and dried. Sometimes the more luxurious salmon and pike were also preserved by salting. Dories, bream and eels were frequently put "in bread", that is, they were baked or boiled in paste. This paste seems to have required eggs, but the way in which it was made is something of a mystery, though the process itself is frequently mentioned. Roger Leyburn even bought his capons in bread, at a slight premium over the usual cost.[5]

The real range of fish available to the medieval household only became apparent when the countess's household moved from Odiham to Dover. There the account lists bar, mackerel, mullet, flounders, salmon, plaice, sole, whelks, cray-fish and crabs. From this it is easy to see why a fifteenth-century schoolboy wrote wistfully: "Wolde to gode I wer on of the dwellers by the see syde, for ther see fysh be plentuse and I love them better than I do this fresh water fysh."[6]

Eggs, cheese and butter also appear with relative frequency among the supplies allotted to the cook. The number of eggs used is particularly striking, especially after the end

F

of Lent, during which their use was forbidden. About a thousand eggs were bought for Easter Sunday, but the ceremony of the Easter egg has a long history and probably not all were intended for cooking. Eggs ranged in price from 3½d to 4½d a hundred, and occasionally a certain number were received as rent. In the week after Easter when eggs were cheap 10s 9½d was spent on them, which would have provided some 3,700. Though the countess's household was somewhat larger than usual that weekend, this number of eggs lasted only till the middle of the following week when they again appeared among the daily purchases.[1] Some medieval recipes called for great numbers of eggs, but they may have been of very small size because of the poor diet of the hens. Frumenty, for example, was a gruel of hulled wheat, boiled with milk and flavoured with various spices; it required one hundred eggs for each eight pints of milk.[2] It was a popular light dish, one of those frequently served for supper.

Cheese and cheese tarts often appeared at the evening meal. Cheese was made everywhere as part of the normal agricultural practice; it was one of the staple provisions for stocking a castle for a siege, or a ship for a long voyage. The softer, more elegant cheeses, such as Brie, appeared in England during the reign of Edward I, but they were only a rare delicacy at the royal table. The countess bought cheese by the poise, or wey, a measure which varied from fourteen to twenty stone.[3] Her officials probably had plenty of experience in choosing the best quality, but when the Goodman of Paris wrote his book of instruction on household management in the fourteenth century he carefully included a rhyme on the subject for his young wife. He wanted to make sure that she would not be easily deceived at market, so he warned her that a good cheese must be:

> Not white as snow, like fair Helen,
> Nor moist like tearful Magdalen,
> Not like Argus, full of eyes,

> But heavy, like a bull of prize,
> Well resisting a thumb pressed in,
> And let it have a scaly skin,
>   Eyeless, and tearless, in colour not white,
>   Scaly, resisting, and weighing not light.[1]

After the heavy emphasis on meat, fish, and eggs, the references to vegetables and fruits seem very meagre indeed. The thirteenth century had no great choice of vegetables, and even those used were not likely to appear on the account if they were grown in the castle garden. Certainly the most common vegetables were dried peas and beans, and they do appear with considerable regularity on the countess's roll. Bartholomew the Englishman mentions beans with ill-concealed dislike in his encyclopaedia, perhaps because they were a standard dish for the friars. He describes beans as having been damned by Pythagoras and says that "by oft use thereof the wits are dulled and [they] cause many dreams".[2] Despite Bartholomew's dislike, the common medieval use of beans and their importance as a source of protein has led one modern scholar to comment that: "In the full sense of the vernacular, the Middle Ages, from the tenth century on, were full of beans."[3]

Onions and garlic were a staple of diet as well as a seasoning. As early as 1237 a covenant was made between the citizens of London and the merchants of Amiens, Corbie and Nesle which provided for free entry of the French garlic and onions, as well as woad for the English cloth dyers.[4] Indeed, from the time of Charlemagne on the French were far more advanced than the English in the use and development of vegetables. Master John of Garland's description of the typical garden of the early thirteenth century was rather more French than English. The list of herbs and vegetables included sage, parsley, fennel, dittany, hyssop, borage, leek, garlic, mustard, onions and porray.*[5] The countess's

---

* Porray was a general term for green vegetables, or potherbs, and was also applied to the soup made from them.

account mentions fennel, parsley, and enormous quantities of mustard. The countess's cook was not alone in his liking for mustard. The Goodman of Paris says that a wedding supper of only forty people would require two quarts of mustard,[1] and Roger Leyburn bought a gallon of mustard at a time.[2]

Fresh fruits are also hard to trace. Apples and pears were naturally the most common. Colin the Marshal bought three hundred pears for the Countess Eleanor at Canterbury when he was there on business at the end of July, and this amount cost only 10d.[3] Pears were probably the most common of all the thirteenth-century fruits, and were frequently grown in the orchard of a castle or manor. Most of the named varieties had been imported from France, and cuttings were used to increase the desired types. The countess's roll also mentions cherries, strawberries, and quinces, while John of Garland in his ideal garden added plums and peaches to the list. Many wild fruits and nuts never appear in the items of the accounts because they were gathered in the nearest wood at no cost. Dried fruits and imported nuts, however, appear in a special place in the roll, as they were reckoned among the spices and bought separately.

A properly constructed garden was a cherished luxury at a castle or wealthy manor. It would have a plot of fine grass, carefully weeded. At the south end would be the fruit trees, and also some climbing vines. There would be plots for aromatic and medicinal herbs, and a few flowers, of which the outstanding favourite was the rose. Medieval men loved flowers; even the sculptors of the cathedrals put flowers in their work, but they were usually the homely flowers of the fields rather than the cultivated blossoms of the rich. Ste-Chapelle is full of buttercups for example, and Notre-Dame in Paris shows plantain, cress and celandine as well.[4] The word orchard was often used to describe the walled garden within the ordinary garden, which the Middle Ages loved so much. The orchard would have fruit trees, but they

84

were not the main reason for its existence. These walled gardens were particularly expensive. The king's instructions for making such gardens at his various castles and manors are very generous, but expense was never a controlling factor for Henry. It is more illuminating to see what the less wealthy did. Henry of Bray, whose estate book gives the cost of his various buildings and improvements, spent 62s 4d in 1297 to make a new herb garden and put walls round it; this was twice the cost of his new kitchen. Six years later, Henry added a dove-cot in the corner of the herb-garden which cost another 46s 8d.[1] Bogo de Clare also made a garden at his wardrobe in London, and listed the expenses in his account: he bought the turf for 3s 10d, and the herbs to plant in it for 10½d; the construction of the garden took one man three weeks, although he had a helper for one week.[2]

The economically minded lord might even make money from his garden by selling his surplus, just as he sold the surplus from his manors. By the end of the century Thomas de Lacy, the earl of Lincoln, had quite an elaborate establishment in Holborn, with a head gardener and several assistants. There was a sufficient quantity of produce to have some for sale, as well as for household use. This garden was large enough to have a fishpond in its centre, and the bailiff had to spend 8s to buy small fish, frogs, and eels to feed the pike in it.[3]

Bread, meat, fish, eggs, cheese, vegetables and fruit – these were, as we might expect, the basic foods, although the relative amounts used were different from our modern pattern. The household accounts are so strictly practical in their listing of the essential commodities that they help to explain *Fleta*'s extraordinarily administrative description of the office of cook. That treatise only insisted that the cook's duty was to render account each day for the number of dishes prepared; nevertheless his place in the household must have depended on his ability to subdue to medieval tastes an overwhelming mass of raw material.

5

The Spice Account

———————◆———————

The ingredients handed to the medieval cook were enormous in amount and relatively limited in interest. Great joints of salted beef, mutton and pork were boiled or roasted for the main midday meal. The fish too was frequently salted, and required considerable effort on the part of the cook if it was to be palatable even to appetites sharpened by continuous life outdoors. The seasonings and luxuries which made this rough fare a little more appetizing, and gave evidence of the householder's worth, were reckoned on the spice account. Since these precious items were far more expensive than the ordinary supplies they were kept locked up in the wardrobe and were only issued to the cook in the amounts required for his immediate needs. Thus the spice account included not only those items now referred to as spices, but also such medieval luxuries as sugar, rice, almonds and dried fruits.

The spice accounts of English households in the thirteenth century were not as extensive as those of France or Italy. A list of "spices" drawn up by a Florentine at the beginning of the fourteenth century to clarify the needs and practices of the merchants mentioned some two hundred and eighty-eight different items, including dye-stuffs, textile fibres, and all the goods which came mainly from the Orient and Africa. A few items from this lengthy list show the extraordinary range of commodities: sheet silver, borax, fresh oranges, pepper, elephant tusks and powdered sugar, to mention only a few.[1] The term "minute spices" was frequently adopted to describe specifically those items sold in small quantities at high prices.

Apart from the domestic interest in how spices were used in medieval cookery, there is the absorbing problem of how these goods finally reached a wealthy household in England. The spice trade has had a long – and somewhat romanticized – history, since for many centuries spices were great luxuries, purchasable only by the rich and important. The profit on them was also extremely high, to counterbalance the undoubted difficulties and dangers of the trade. The great change in the pattern of the spice trade did not come till the end of the fifteenth century when the Europeans first began to explore the African coast for themselves, and finally found their way to India and the Spice Islands. This new development profoundly changed the character of the commerce, which till then had followed a plan elaborated over many centuries. Masefield's description of the quinquireme of Nineveh applied also to much of the medieval period, though the Indian and Arab spice traders, and the Italian merchants who bought from them, carried many more goods.

The details of the trade routes which brought the coveted spices and Oriental luxuries to western Europe are still considerably disputed. It was a trade of many intermediate stages and innumerable middlemen which continually adapted itself to changing conditions. Normally the traders sought the most convenient overseas route so as to avoid the higher cost and greater dangers of overland transport. Arabia was the pivot of much of this trade, and its maritime commerce was almost totally concentrated on Aden. The Indian and Chinese ships – some of which were large and sufficiently seaworthy to make the journey from Fu-Kim to Arabia in sixty days – came mainly to Aden. They brought valuable cargoes, not only from China but also from Indo-China and the Malabar Coast. At Aden the Indian and Chinese merchants usually transferred their cargoes to smaller ships whose pilots knew the Red Sea, or sold their goods immediately to Arab merchants. Once the Red Sea had been safely navigated, the goods were transferred to camel back to reach the Nile, and from there were floated downstream to Alexandria.

There was a general ignorance in the thirteenth century of the actual stages of the spice trade, which is amusingly illustrated by Joinville's* description of the Nile. The great river impressed the French knight mightily, for he thought it came from the Earthly Paradise, and brought the spices with it.

> Before the river enters into Egypt, people who are accustomed so to do, cast their nets out-spread into the river, at night; and when morning comes, they find in their nets such goods as are sold by weight, and brought into the land, viz., ginger, rhubarb, wood of aloes, and cinnamon. And it is said that these things come from the earthly paradise, just as the wind blows down the dry wood in the forests of our own land; and the dry wood of the trees in paradise that thus falls into the river is sold to us by the merchants.[1]

Despite his fanciful idea of the origin of these valuable commodities, Joinville realized very early that Alexandria was the most important town in the Egypt of his day and deserved its description as "the market of two worlds". Indeed during the thirteenth century Egypt was the trading centre where western merchants found it easiest to buy eastern goods; Acre challenged Egypt's position during the conflicts between the Moslems and the Crusader states but never succeeded in superseding it.

From the Levantine markets, and pre-eminently from Alexandria, the western merchants carried their rich cargoes back to Europe. At this period the spice merchants were predominantly Italian, for the Italians were the great entrepreneurs of the luxury trade. The Venetians were already particularly prominent; by the fourteenth century

---

* Joinville (c. 1228–1318) was the friend and biographer of St Louis, the great king of France. Both his attitudes and his knowledge were typical of his age and knightly class, and his *Life of St Louis* is a useful personal interpretation of his times.

they were annually sending their galleys out of the Mediterranean and up the Channel to England and Flanders. This allowed them to tap the profits directly, and their ships brought an exotic appearance to Southampton's harbour. But during the thirteenth century the spices, as well as all the other luxuries for England, generally came overland from Italy for distribution at the great fairs of Champagne. The English spice and silk merchants were dealing with goods many steps removed from their place of origin.

The countess of Leicester's account does not always specify where the purchases which appear on her account were made; but it appears to be true for the Leicester household, as well as for those others whose records have survived, that the more unusual and expensive items were bought in London, while such common spices as pepper and ginger were more widely available. There is no evidence that the countess made her purchases at the great fairs of Winchester or Boston, as Bishop Grosseteste had advised the countess of Lincoln to do,[1] but even in 1265 the usual channels of trade were sufficiently undisturbed to make the purchase of spices still a matter of course. The effects of civil war did not totally disrupt commerce or seriously affect the price of commodities. The account of Roger Leyburn emphasizes this fact since it shows that he bought cloves, saffron, ginger, cinnamon and pepper at the usual prices while he was subduing the Cinque Ports for the king.[2]

If we turn to a closer examination of the particular spices and herbs listed in these thirteenth-century accounts, we get a clearer idea of their relative expense and their individual place in the recipes of the day. The most common of all spices was pepper. Although the thirteenth-century cooks used it frequently and it figures on all the lists of spices, even the learned men did not understand where it came from or how it grew. Bartholomew the Englishman had a most ingenious explanation of the way in which it was grown and harvested. He claimed that pepper was the seed of a tree which grew in the strong sun on the south side of a hill in the Caucasus. The woods there were infested with serpents, so when the pepper was ripe the inhabitants set fire to the woods to chase off the snakes. With this extraordinary piece of natural history Bartholomew triumphantly accounted for the difference between black and white pepper, for "by such burning the grain of pepper that was naturally white was made black".[1] In sober fact, pepper is black when the berry has been dried in the sun without removing the skin, and white when skinned before drying. White pepper was not well known in the west during the Middle Ages. The Arabs knew that pepper grew on the Malabar Coast, and they bought it at Seraf or Aden; from there it passed through Egypt in the usual manner, and the Venetians monopolized the greater part of the trade in western Europe.

In the countess's account, the price of pepper fluctuates wildly, from 10d to 2s 4d a pound.[2] The normal cost seems to have been about 10d, and later in the century it dropped as low as 7d.[3] At this rate the many people who held land for a rent of a pound of pepper a year must have profited from the drop in price.

Another common spice, almost as much in use as pepper, was ginger. It was widely grown in India and on the Malabar Coast; there was also a superior variety which was sold in the market of Mecca and came to Europe by way of Alexandria. A careful manager, such as the Goodman of Paris, distinguished between the two kinds of ginger; that which came from the Malabar Coast was known as "colombine", while that from Mecca was "string" ginger. The Goodman felt that Mecca ginger was far superior to the other, and indeed in his day it was always more expensive.[4]

Ginger had been a popular spice even in Roman times, and was much used in medieval sauces; as in the Goodman's recipe for cameline, where ginger was mixed with cinnamon, saffron, and nutmeg, as well as breadcrumbs and brown sugar.[5] Besides being used extensively in the kitchen, ginger was a valuable part of the apothecary's stock; it would be used by the lady of the house to treat the ills of her household as it had a warming and opiate effect. The price of ginger, like that of pepper, varies widely in the countess of Leicester's account, from 10d to 2s 6d.[1] The fluctuations in price were less extreme at the end of the century and may perhaps be explained by carriage charges. Bishop Swinfield of Hereford paid 1s 1d a pound for his ginger, but Bogo de Clare, much nearer to the London market, only 10d.[2] There is even mention of gingerbread, but it was an expensive luxury since it cost 3s a pound.[3]

Cinnamon was both popular and relatively easy to obtain. It had been imported into France as early as the beginning of the eighth century, when it was sufficiently rare to make a most acceptable present. Its place of origin is no longer known, but during the Middle Ages it was certainly found in China, and also on the coasts of India and Indo-China. It was plentiful in the markets of Alexandria, a fact which lent colour to Joinville's tale that it had floated downstream from the earthly Paradise. Bartholomew the Englishman reports an even more far-fetched explanation for the source of cinnamon. He mentions an old tale that cinnamon was found in the nests of birds, especially those of the phoenix, and that the birds must be shot down with lead arrows in order to capture the spice; but, he adds sternly, this was only deception to make it more expensive.[4] Two terms, cannella and cinnamon, were used to describe the spice; at first they were considered interchangeable, but by the fifteenth century cinnamon was considered the finer and more precious. The countess's cinnamon was reasonable in price, ranging only from 10d to 1s, and this price range remained standard throughout the century.

Like ginger, cloves, which had been imported into France by the time of the Merovingians, were extensively used in medicines as well as in cooking and aromatic drinks; but they always remained expensive. The countess bought them in small amounts, a pound or a half pound at a time – compared to six pounds of cinnamon – and she paid as much as 13s a pound for them.[1] Cloves must have been particularly expensive in 1265, for they are listed in later thirteenth-century accounts at only 2s a pound.[2] They were a common ingredient in medieval recipes; but since medieval cooks rarely mention measurements, even approximate ones, it is hard to estimate the amount of cloves used compared with other less expensive seasonings such as ginger and cinnamon.

Another aromatic root, resembling ginger, was galingale. Its fame had been spread by the writings of the Arab doctors who prized it as a drug because of its heating effect and it was used widely in medieval Europe. It was also used in cooking, and cost considerably less than cloves. The countess paid 18d a pound for galingale, a price which varied little through the rest of the century.[3] There were different qualities; the best came from China, and the poorer kind from the south of Asia, whence it found its way to the usual eastern markets. The Goodman of Paris* tried to help his wife to choose the proper quality, and explained that the galingale which has the reddest violet colour when cut was the better. It should also be heavy and firm to the knife, he added, for sometimes it was spoilt, mouldy, and as light as dead wood.[4]

There are a few other spices mentioned in one or another of the accounts although they were never as commonly used as the ones already described. Zedoary, for example, was another of the aromatic gingery substances made from the roots of an East Indian plant. It was particularly useful for medicine and perfumery, and was among the most expensive costing 2s for a half pound.[5] Mace, made from the dried delicate shell of the nutmeg, and cubebs, a spicy Javanese berry somewhat resembling pepper, were used to flavour sugar and wine.[6]

* See below, page 82.

Apart from spices, there were also several herbs which played a prominent part in the spice account. Of these, saffron was extremely expensive, while anise and fennel were common and cheap. Mustard and parsley, which are also properly herbs, were most frequently grown in the castle garden, or were available at the nearest market at a very low price. For this reason, they appear among the daily reckonings rather than among the more valuable items kept under lock and key.

Saffron was the most important, as it was the most costly, of all the herbs. Though it was originally from the east, it had been acclimatized in Spain by the tenth century, and figured prominently in the thirteenth century trade of Spain with England. It comes from the saffron crocus; only the stigmas of the flowers are used, and it takes about 75,000 flowers to make one pound of saffron. It cost the countess of Leicester between 10s. and 14s a pound on the occasions when she purchased it.[1] She never bought more than a pound, but a very little saffron goes a very long way. Despite the price it was a popular ingredient in many medieval sauce recipes, and even had its own terminology. According to the Goodman of Paris, the well-instructed cook spoke of garnishing a dish with parsley, but fringing it with saffron.[2]

Cummin was a popular and inexpensive spice from the herb *cyminum* which was grown in many herb gardens. Although it only cost the countess 2d a pound, Bogo de Clare had to pay as much as 8d or 10d for his supply.[3] Cummin was much used as a spice for flavouring poultry. Indeed when the English queen sailed to France in the spring of 1254, the sheriff of Sussex was ordered to prepare for her voyage thirty dozen chickens, thirty dozen fowl, and four thousand of cummin![4] The Middle Ages had a great affection for a truly spicy sauce, but this would seem a liberal quantity for the most jaded palate. Cummin is still used for flavouring, though not normally in such quantities; it has an important place in curry powder, and also in kummel.

Anise and fennel are other herbs from the Middle Ages that are still used: anise chiefly in liqueurs such as anisette and absinthe, though in the Middle Ages it was also employed in meat jellies; fennel for flavouring fish, and in salads. Fennel was also used medicinally in medieval households. According to the herbalists, it not only comforted the stomach but counteracted dropsy, increased a woman's milk, and was a remedy for mistiness of the eyes and worms in the ears.[1] The countess bought anise and fennel at 3d a pound while her household was in Dover;[2] probably their purchase was a necessity because Dover castle did not have the usual castle garden with its variety of herbs.

Coriander was another herb in general use and Bishop Swinfield records its purchase for his household[3] at a cost of 4d a pound. The coriander seeds were used for flavouring wines, preserves, and even meat dishes; herbalists recommend their use with honey to slay worms.[4] Although coriander is now used in pickles and curry powder, it has lost much of its old position.

From the medieval recipes that have come down to us, it is obvious that the cook used all the available spices freely. The most vivid description of the astonishing number of spices taken for granted in daily living is to be found in the recipe of the Goodman of Paris for a special preserve, of which the basis was nuts, turnips, carrots, choke-pears, pumpkins, and peaches. Incidentally this preserve was not a matter lightly begun, since the cook was adjured to start working with the nuts on St John's day (June 24th), and it was not till St Andrew's day (November 30th) that he had come to the end of his list of ingredients and could begin their combination with the spices. For each five hundred nuts the cook was to take a pound of mustard seed, half a pound of anise, and a quarter and a half each of fennel, coriander, and caraways, pounded and soaked in vinegar.

The cook then put into this mixture half a pound of horse-radish, half a quarter* each of cloves, cinnamon, pepper, ginger, nutmeg, grain of Paradise, as well as half an ounce of saffron and an ounce of red cedar. All this spicy base, with two pounds of mashed raisins, were to be added with wine and vinegar to twelve pounds of honey and well cooked.

Despite the medieval fondness for spicy dishes, it is reasonable to wonder whether the problems of transport, storage and refining did not seriously affect the quality of spices available to them. It seems likely that a great quantity was needed to achieve even a moderate result. Nevertheless it is easy to understand why the mortar and pestle were dominant items in the medieval kitchen. The sound of the pounding required to render usable these large quantities of spices must have been a constant accompaniment to the other kitchen noises. Bogo de Clare's account mentions specifically that he had his purchase of spices pounded at the merchant's place of business before the various powders were sorted into sheepskin pouches and then enclosed in a sack for dispatch to Thatcham; but this practice must have been unusual, for it added considerably to the cost. A contemporary song underlines the daily necessity of such a chore, for the pedlar, who had been cataloguing his wares to an attentive audience, tried to persuade the listening women to pay with money, or with iron, or even with eggs, for some of his goods so that the little maids could get back to their mortars.

Besides spices the less expensive varieties of sugar had to be pounded. Sugar was normally reckoned on the spice account because it was an expensive addition to the medieval diet. It used to be thought that sugar was unknown until later in the Middle Ages, and that only honey was employed for sweetening; but a close study of the accounts shows that sugar was in continuous use in wealthy households by the

* Although the recipe does not specifically say so, it would seem that a quarter and a half meant $\frac{3}{8}$ of a pound, and half a quarter, $\frac{1}{8}$.

middle of the thirteenth century. The countess's account mentions both ordinary sugar, which may be presumed to be the less expensive loaf type, and powdered white sugar. Sugar was 1s a pound in April, but the price had risen to 2s by the end of July.[1] Although its cost was not exorbitant the quantities mentioned are not very large. Over the whole seven months of the account only some fifty-five pounds are reckoned, while over the same period the countess bought fifty-three pounds of pepper. Further sweetening probably came from honey, made by bees kept within the precincts of castle or manor, and thus not in evidence on the roll.

Sugar cane was grown in Syria by the tenth century. From there it spread into Egypt, North Africa, Spain, and Sicily. The early crusaders first encountered sugar cane in Tripoli and loved to suck on it. Certainly it was their knowledge of and demand for sugar when they returned to Europe which helped to encourage the importation of refined sugar. Until the fall of the Latin kingdoms, Damascus was the centre of the sugar market. The Syrians not only cultivated sugar cane, they had also learned how to extract the juice, concentrate it over the fire and then to dry it slowly to make sugar. The lowest quality of refined sugar was the loaf which the later Italian merchants insisted should be "white, dry, and a well-compacted paste".[2] By the end of the thirteenth century, when Venice had begun to send the Flanders galleys on their yearly voyage, the ships' cargoes also included brown sugar and molasses from Sicily, as well as refined sugar from that island which had been growing sugar cane for some time.[3] Powdered sugar was a great luxury, and was often flavoured with some spice or aromatic flower; the countess bought powdered sugar flavoured with mace, and Bogo de Clare jars of rose and violet sugars.[4] These are a great deal more exotic than the rather extreme modern practice of flavouring sugar with vanilla beans or cinnamon sticks.

Many of these fancy sugars were particularly popular as

4. Dover Castle: Newel Stairs in the north-east tower of the keep

5a. Cook using a flesh-hook to remove meat from a cauldron
From the *Maciejowski Bible*, M638 f.20

5b. Dinner at the high table
From the *Maciejowski Bible*, M638 f.37v

medicines. The Arab doctors recommended sugar for the chest, and their prescriptions were copied by the English and French medical men. The wardrobe account of Edward I's son Henry shows this very clearly. Henry must have been a delicate boy who suffered from many colds for his account is full of references to rose and violet sugar, as well as *penidia* which was made into little twisted sticks like modern barley sugar. When Master Hugh of Evesham, the visiting physician, came to treat Henry, he not only ordered sugar and sugar syrups, but also liquorice for cooking with the water Henry drank.[1] It is sad to note that all the sugars and sweet concoctions helped Henry no more than the thirteen widows who watched in prayer all night at Guildford for his recovery. Many candles were also made to his measure – a tiny one, for they only required two pounds of wax – and were set to burn at all the famous shrines; but they could not help the sickly boy avoid an early death in October 1274.[2] More robust invalids might be given their sugar in a chicken mould, one of the Goodman's suggestions for an excellent pottage for the sick. It calls for a "great plenty of sugar" with the boiled and pounded chicken, but surprisingly no spices.[3] Some people seem to have had a sweeter tooth than others. The accounts of Bishop Swinfield's household, for example, mention the purchase of more than one hundred pounds of sugar – mostly in the coarse loaves – and also of liquorice and twelve pounds of sweetmeats.[4]

Today we think of sugar and salt as complementary flavourings for food, and our domestic accounts would show a great predominance of sugar. This was not so in the Middle Ages, and it is easy to underestimate the quantities of salt required in the medieval household. The emphasis in their diet on salted meat and fish, and also on the use of brine or souse for pickling, called for generous amounts of salt in the kitchen. It was a common necessity, so frequently purchased that price records can be kept with almost the same regularity as those for grain.

Salt was bought by the quarter or the bushel, from overseas as well as from domestic sources. During the thirteenth century some salt was imported from the famous saltpans of the Bay of Bourgneuf near the island of Oléron, but "Bay salt" had not yet reached the commanding position it later occupied in the salt trade of Europe. Larger quantities came from the domestic suppliers: either the salt mines, such as those in Worcestershire, or the simple salt-works along the coast which relied on the principle of evaporation. At least by the end of the century, if not before, salt was processed on the lands of Isabella de Fortibus at Lymington, not too far from Odiham.[1]

Since salt was a necessary commodity its price remained fairly low, though transport costs added to its price inland. It has been suggested that the fluctuations in its price were due mainly to the amount of sunshine each year; wet years meant expensive salt. During the '60s the average price of salt in England varied between 3d and 5d a bushel; Roger Leyburn, for example, paid 3d a bushel.[2] However, the countess of Leicester seems to have had difficulty obtaining supplies in Dover. During July, she bought ten quarters of salt from a Sandwich merchant at the high price of 44s 6d, about 6½d a bushel, and then had to rent a ship at 2s 6d to bring this supply back to Dover.[3]

The spice account also listed such items as rice which, as an imported delicacy, was kept under lock and key. Rice was another important element in the English trade with Spain in the thirteenth century. The countess used one hundred and ten pounds from Christmas to April, at a cost of about 1½d a pound.[4] A fourteenth-century cookery book suggests that rice should be used as a side dish with meat, or in a "blank-manger" with chicken meat, milk of almonds and fried almonds.[5]

This combinations of almonds and rice is a frequent one, since almonds play an important part in many medieval recipes. They were relatively cheap, and another staple of the Anglo-Spanish trade. Besides being used in cooking, they were often blanched and served as dessert with dried fruits. The amounts used were very large; Edward's royal household used 28,500 pounds of almonds in 1286, as compared with 6,600 pounds of rice.[1] The countess bought 280 pounds of almonds during the period of the roll, and 5 pounds cost only 1s.[2] Almonds seem to have had still another use, as a cosmetic. King Edward's ten-year-old daughter, Eleanor, was provided twice with almond and violet oil for her own special use.[3]

Dried fruits were also listed; dates, raisins and figs were the main varieties known in England in the thirteenth century. In the earlier years of the century these supplies frequently came from Spain; later the Flanders galleys of the Venetians absorbed more and more of this profitable trade. Some fruit also came overland from Italy, and was bought at the great fairs of Champagne. Raisins and figs were often packed in "frails", baskets made of rushes but of no fixed size – a fact which makes it difficult to compare accounts intelligently. However, Roger Leyburn bought his raisins and figs by the pound; raisins cost him 2d a pound, and figs 1½d.[4] A special luxury turns up on the account of Bogo de Clare, with the mention of two pomegranates for the extraordinary sum of 12d,[5] but this was obviously a new and extremely expensive fruit. Fresh fruit was also served for dessert, but were never included on the spice account because they were reckoned on the daily account for the kitchen.

In some household accounts of this time the purchases of wax were grouped together in a special account or, as in Bishop Swinfield's roll, they are listed with the spices. The countess of Leicester's purchases of wax, however, are rather casually handled by the clerk; they are sometimes listed with the spices, sometimes mentioned on the front of a membrane after a daily accounting. Wax had three main uses: it was needed in the chapel for the candles which burned during mass; for domestic lighting in wealthy households; and a fairly large quantity was required for the sealing of letters and legal documents, since without a proper seal the authenticity of any medieval communication was suspect.

Large quantities of wax were used in the countess's household. Thus, in seven weeks eight pounds were required for the chapel, thirty-eight pounds for the household, and fifty-four pounds were sent to Amaury.[1] Though there is no record for the darkest months of the year, the household seems to have consistently used about a pound of wax a day. This suggests only one large candle, probably for the high table at supper, as one of the requirements of the abbot of Westminster's tenant was to provide two wax candles for the abbot on his visit. Each of these candles was to be of one pound of wax – apparently a standard size – and, in accord with his usual perquisite, the chamberlain had the benefit of the candle ends.[2] During the period of the account, the proportion of wax required for the chapel, as compared to that for the household, remains about the same, and the countess would often make gifts of wax to priests or friars.[3] Although these amounts of wax are carefully recorded, there is no mention of purchases or cost. It would appear that the countess had followed the advice laid down by Bishop Grosseteste in his *Rules*, to make the necessary purchases of wax only twice a year.[4] Her yearly supply must have been laid in before the surviving fragment of the roll began, and the clerk's duty was merely to provide an accounting of how much had been used to tally later against the remaining supply. This system of twice yearly purchases seems to have been followed by Bishop Swinfield who had his official buy supplies in London about Epiphany, and again about Whitsuntide. The bishop's household required three hundred and sixty-two pounds for a yearly supply,[5] again an average of about a pound a day. His wax cost him about 5d a pound, but in the '60s the average price was 6d; obviously too expensive for any but the rich. These good wax candles had cotton for the wick, while poorer candles were made of tallow.[1]

Yet candles were not the only source of light. Rush-lights were the only lighting available for the poor, and were also used by the wealthy to supplement other lights. These bulrushes, dipped in tallow and then set alight, have been casting a rather faint glimmer from almost the first pages of recorded history. Brighter than the rush-light was the cresset lamp, which was filled with oil or melted tallow and had several cotton wicks. These lamps were often highly ornate, far more elegant even than the great candlesticks that dominated any room in which they were placed. Candlesticks were usually of the pricket type, that is there was a spike in the base of the candlestick on which the candle was impaled, and they came in many sizes. King Henry, who was always anxious for convenience as well as beauty in the royal palaces, sought to make improvements in their lighting. In one of his detailed building instructions he ordered that shelves should be built in the chamber of the Lord Edward and of the king's brother at Clarendon, so that lights could be placed there.[2] Such shelves would have double usefulness, for they could accommodate either small candlesticks or standing cresset lamps.

Wax, fruit, sugar, herbs and spices – all these added charm to the life of the wealthy in the Middle Ages, and their detailed listing in the thirteenth-century accounts shows just what was available to them. It is interesting that despite the confusion of civil war the normal channels of the luxury trade remained open. In the period covered by the accounts of the countess of Leicester and Roger Leyburn there was certainly an increase in some prices, but no signs of big shortages or profiteering. Of course they were both in specially favoured positions. It may have been their particular good fortune to have the ordinary routine of their purchases continue with so little upheaval, but the valuable imports were still available; the merchants carried on their usual trade despite unsettled conditions.

6

Wine and Beer

———◆———

Since there was so much ginger and other equally hot spices in almost every dish, even the hardened medieval palate must have needed large quantities to drink. Their standard drinks were wine and beer; wine for the upper classes and the honoured guests, and beer for the ordinary members of the household or as a casual drink. Water was disdained, a natural reaction to the exposed nature of most medieval wells and their frequent pollution. Bartholomew the English-man discussed the dangers of cold water most forcefully; he was convinced that it made you ill, especially in old age. Warm water he reluctantly allowed, since it was a help to those who had colic in the night;[1] but Bartholomew's real enthusiasm was for wine. He declared emphatically that wine when "moderately drunk most comforteth the body, and gladdeth the heart, and saveth wounds and evils".[2]

Other less important beverages are occasionally mentioned, but not in large quantities. Milk was normally used only in cooking, though young Henry's account shows quite a large amount of milk bought for the children.[3] Bartholomew dealt seriously with the nature of milk, since his purpose was to define almost everything. So far as milk was concerned he was not satisfied to dismiss it in general remarks; he took eight separate chapters to discuss the qualities and enumerate the individual virtues of the milk of camels, goats, cows, sheep, asses, mares, pigs, and finally – vaguely – "animals".[4]

Cider was made and drunk, depending on the availability of apples, and the quantities mentioned are small. Two of the earl of Cornwall's manors, Cippenham and Isleworth, account for cider made from apples of their own gardens, but the largest amount mentioned is only fourteen tuns.[*1] The countess of Leicester's roll lists the use of one tun of cider at a single dinner for the poor, although the clerk adds that there were eight hundred present.[2] In 1260 a tun of cider cost only 5s; by the end of the century the price had risen to 8s or 9s.[3] Despite the romantic emphasis on mead as a favourite medieval drink only one mention of it appears in these thirteenth-century accounts, for the household of Bishop Swinfield of Hereford.[4] The implication is that it was a rather old-fashioned drink, still occasionally used in the country but not popular among the more fashionable members of the baronial class.

Wine was the choice, not only of the upper classes, but of all who could afford it. General use did not preclude over-indulgence, and there is ample evidence that the heavy drinker, with his jaundiced distaste for the morning after, was also a familiar figure in the Middle Ages. Rutebeuf, the popular French poet of the thirteenth century, satirized the medieval form of drunken bragging when he explained that after an evening with plenty of wine and a warm fire all the knights were full of fervour for the crusade, and boasted of their prowess against the sultan and his men; but in the cold light of morning these night-time warriors had "changed their Latin" and given up the crusade for the easier game of hares and ducks.[5]

Others besides the poets bear witness to the common acceptance of wine in the household, and some of the ills that arose from its excessive use. Salimbene† has quite a long, though incidental, discussion on the virtues and dangers of wine. He summarized the general medieval attitude,

* The reckoning of a tun is discussed below; see p. 110.
† Salimbene was an Italian Franciscan of the thirteenth century who wrote a gossipy, anecdotal chronicle of his wandering Franciscan life in Italy and France.

and also mentioned an unusual superstition which the Franciscans seem to have rejected with robust good sense. Salimbene wrote of the different attitudes towards wine of the various races:

> So the French delight in good wine, nor need we wonder, for wine "cheereth God and man", as it is written in the ninth chapter of Judges. . . . It may be said literally that French and English make it their business to drink full goblets. Wherefore the French have bloodshot eyes; for from their ever-free potations of wine their eyes become red-rimmed and bleared and bloodshot. And in the early morning after they have slept off their wine, they go with such eyes to the priest who has celebrated mass, and pray him to drop into their eyes the water wherein he has washed his hands.

The friar went on to corroborate the truth of the English reputation for hard drinking, but he added charitably: "Yet we must forgive the English if they are glad to drink wine when they can, for they have but little wine in their own country".[1]

England had always imported much of its wine, despite the mention of local vineyards as far back as Domesday Book. There were still occasional references to English wines in the chronicles and accounts of the thirteenth century. Bishop Swinfield, for example, had a vineyard at his manor of Ledbury; he took seven tuns of white wine, and almost another tun of verjuice, from it in 1290.[2] The officials of the earl of Cornwall carefully account for the expenses incurred in taking care of the vines at Isleworth and Wallingford, but they only received three tuns and one pipe of wine from Isleworth.[3] Unless the English climate of these years was much warmer and sunnier than today wine made from home-grown grapes would be scanty, and probably rather bitter. Even in Anglo-Saxon times wine was normally imported, generally brought in from Rouen, although there was also a small trade in German wines. By the beginning of the thirteenth century there was a change in the kind of wine drunk and in the district from which it came.

When Henry II married Eleanor of Aquitaine her rich heritage included several of the great wine districts of France, whose vintages began to come freely to the English market. Surprisingly enough, the excellent wines of Anjou were never very successful in the English trade. Until the end of the twelfth century the wines from Poitou were the most favoured; they were shipped in large quantities from La Rochelle. But this trade, as well as the privileges of Rouen in the market of London, was suppressed after King John's loss of Poitou and Normandy. John acted to counterbalance the ensuing deficiencies in the wine trade by making concessions to Bordeaux, the centre of English power in Gascony. The first cargo of Gascon wine came to Southampton in 1213, and to Bristol the following year.[1] These were the precursors of a mighty fleet: from the beginning of the thirteenth century on, Gascon wine ruled supreme in the markets of England, although much confusion and shortage was caused by the Hundred Years War.

The wine trade between England and Gascony was of such great value that both sides depended heavily on it. The Gascons turned the whole district around Bordeaux to vines, at the expense of everything else, in the hope of further increasing their profits. When Simon de Montfort was the king's lieutenant in Gascony he could deal the rebellious Gascons no harsher blow than to cut their vines. Gascony's vines even took over the land needed for the production of essential cereals, and thus Gascony came to depend on England for its grain. This dependence was so great that special arrangements were made to continue the export of grain to Gascony even in times of lean harvest in England. As well as importing grain, the Gascons provided a profitable market for English cloth.

Bordeaux was not only a wine-growing district, it was also the port for the many inland wines shipped in small boats, on the Garonne, the Tarn, and the Lot. Yet the bourgeoisie of Bordeaux did not want the profits on their wines endangered by their neighbours. They acquired exemption from the heaviest export duty, as well as the privilege that wine from up-country could not be sold till after November 11th. This allowed the Bordeaux wine to sell out first without competition, and at a good price. This early sale was particularly important since the wine trade was a seasonal affair, based on the transport of the new vintage to England as rapidly as possible.

The harvest was pressed in September and was ready for export in October. Late in September, all kinds of ships gathered in Bordeaux harbour to await their cargo. Probably the ships of Bayonne were the most numerous, for this city had the greatest share of the carrying trade; but there were also ships from the Basque country, from Oléron and La Rochelle, as well as a few manned by Bretons, Normans, and the English themselves. Bordeaux itself concentrated on growing wine, rather than providing ships for its carriage. The waiting ships filled their holds with the casks as quickly as possible. The earlier they could leave, the better the sailing weather, and the earliest arrival demanded premium prices. There was also a spring wine fleet, which took what might be left over of the Bordeaux harvest, as well as the inland wine. These ship captains tried to get back to England for the Easter feasts, but some left as late as May or June.

Medieval wine had a short life, usually a year or less; there was no emphasis on vintages in the modern sense. If the harvest was good, the price went down a little; some chronicler might notice a particularly good season, but there was no comparison of "wine years". The medieval vintners recognized the danger of air making the wine acid, and they tried their best to produce well-cared-for wines, but they could not make them keep. By summer the old wine was almost undrinkable. Sometimes the early grapes, which were not fully ripe, were pressed to make verjuice, a sharp liquid from the green fruit. It could be made in July and, since it was considered less heating, it was often used in summer instead of wine; but verjuice travelled poorly, and many of the English and French cooks used whatever was available from their local grapes. The freshly pressed, unfermented juice of the mature grapes was known as 'must'. This had to be left in the cask to 'boil', or ferment, but as soon as the scum had risen and been skimmed off, the head could be put on the cask and the resultant product described as new wine. Must was occasionally shipped to England, but the greatest quantity of imports was made up of new wine.

The ships of the autumn fleet arrived at English ports between October and January; some of them carried fairly large cargoes. In 1266 a dozen ships from Bayonne, San Sebastian, and Fuenterrabia brought four hundred and sixty-five casks of wine to the Cinque Port of Winchelsea in Christmas week.[1] Bristol, Southampton, London, Hull, and Sandwich were the main wine ports, but the ships also came in smaller numbers to many others. So much of the shipping trade was engaged in the handling of wine casks, each of which occupied sixty cubic feet in the hold of a ship, that the number of tuns a ship could carry became the universally accepted measure of a vessel's capacity, or tonnage. The wine brought by the spring fleet was often referred to as 'rack' wine; it had time to settle before shipment and had been drawn off the lees, or racked. The word 'rack' passed into English from this Gascon term, yet another testimony to the influence of the Gascon wine trade.

Certain elements of the thirteenth-century wine trade can be described with some precision, but it is impossible to estimate the exact amounts involved since a sufficient number of continuous accounts does not appear until the fourteenth century. Nevertheless there can be no doubt that wine played a very much larger part in the economy of the time than is often realized. By the middle of the fifteenth century, when statistics begin to mean something, England was importing some three million gallons of wine a year – one-third of the value of her whole import trade.[1] Although the exact figures would not hold good for the thirteenth century, it is not unlikely that the same proportion could be observed.[2]

Because of the large amount of wine imported, the royal "prise" was a valuable right. By this custom, the royal officials had the right to take for the king's use one cask from every ship carrying ten or more, and two casks from every ship carrying twenty or more. Occasionally the king would exempt certain ships from the prise as a mark of special favour. The author of *Fleta* specified briefly that these prisage wines were to be taken one "at the ship's prow and another at the poop",[3] in other words, not merely from the very best wines which were usually stored together in one part of the ship.

The king's butler, who was in charge of the royal prise, was interested in several kinds of wine. He would purchase the finest available for the king's table, a good quality for the royal household, and a large quantity of cheap wine to provision the royal castles. Prices naturally fluctuated in relation to the quantity and quality of the vintage, and the time when the wine shipments arrived in bulk. Prisage wines were paid for at the flat rate of 20s a tun, and the large number of entries about wine in the Liberate Rolls suggest that the average market price for wine during Henry III's reign was £2 a tun. Another factor which strongly influenced the price of wine was the cost of transport, for carriage charges inland or cross-country added considerably to the basic price.

Although the king was the greatest purchaser of wine, it was common practice for a great magnate such as the earl of Leicester to make special arrangements for the importation of the large quantities he required. As early as 1247 the Countess Eleanor had a licence for the import of twenty-four tuns on the ship of Aimery Durant.[4] During the period that the earl of Leicester was the king's lieutenant in Gascony he had his own ship bringing wines to England,[1] and this arrangement apparently continued after he left. In 1255 the keepers of the king's wines at Southampton were ordered not to take for the king's use any of the wines which Columbus de Burg brought for the use of Simon de Montfort.[2]

Despite the many references to the arrival of wines at the various ports and the amounts bought or taken by prise, the tracing of their further distribution inland is not easy The evidence is fragmentary, but it is fair to say that there was an adequate supply of carts to transport these wine casks all over England, awkward and cumbersome though the loads must have been. Sometimes the carts and their drivers belonged to the manors of the lord for whom they carried, but there were also groups of carts for hire in the larger towns and a regular business of providing rented transport was carried on. The average rate seems to have been 1d per tun per mile for a journey which could be done in a day.[3]

The amounts of wine mentioned in the countess of Leicester's account vary considerably, and are not always in direct relation to the number of people served. In the first part of the roll when the countess and her household were at Odiham, their use of wine was quite restrained; the normal daily allowance varied between one and two sesters, or sextaries. Eighteen and a half sesters were recorded on March 19th, but this was the day the earl arrived with a company so large that three hundred and thirty-four horses were fed in the stable. Even that quantity of wine was not sufficient for the assembly, as they also bought two hundred and forty gallons of beer.[4] Late in the summer, at Dover castle, very large amounts of wine appear on the account. These no doubt reflect the number of men on castleguard, but they also illustrate what happened when the normal processes of brewing or buying beer were no longer possible. In the week of August 16th, the clerk accounted daily for a quarter of a tun of Gascon wine for the knights, and half a tun of bastard wine for the household.[1] These quantities seem astoundingly large when there were fewer than thirty horses in the stable.

However, despite the apparent precision of the amounts listed daily by the clerk, it is impossible to be sure to what actual quantities they refer on each occasion because of the curiously variable nature of medieval weights and measures. According to the usual reckoning, the tun contained two hundred and fifty-two gallons, and there were sixty-three sesters to the tun, each containing four gallons. On the other hand *Fleta* asserted that a tun of wine contained only fifty-two sesters, with each sester still made up of four gallons;[2] this reckoning resulted in a tun of only two hundred and eight gallons. Besides the confusion over the tun, there was further lack of consistency in the size of the sester. A sester of sweet wine was only two gallons, while a sester of ale could be as much as twelve or fourteen. Such extreme variations may have had their origin in the idea that the sester represented a weekly allowance; thus disparities in amount might represent the different types of liquid measured.[3] The confident language of the clerk and the assize conceal the fact that any generalization based on such constantly varying measures can be little more than an informed guess.

The responsible official of the household was plagued with several problems about the provision of wine. He not only had to be sure that each of the castles or manors in which the household resided had a sufficient supply for the period of its stay, but also to consider the different types of wine and try to satisfy the lord's preference. The first entries on the countess of Leicester's roll speak only of wine, but the later ones define whether it was red or white, Gascon or bastard. Just as the medieval cooks served foods which were highly spiced, so the medieval butlers served wines which were mixed or spiced or sweetened. Bastard, for example, was merely the term applied to all mixed and sweetened wines, and there were many of these. Thus for Christmas 1249 Ralph de Roketon was ordered to make for the king clarry, which was sweetened with honey and spices, piment, also spiced, as well as two sesters of wine flavoured with zedoary, two or three with nutmegs, and two with cubebs.[1]

There were medicated wines as well as those that were sweetened and spiced. At the beginning of the fourteenth century a very popular text was written by an eminent physician, Arnald of Villanova, on the many varieties of medicated wines and the diseases against which they protected the drinker. His text describes the means and methods of spicing wines for these helpful purposes. Among the most efficient, he felt, were raisin wine, clove wine, anise wine and, above all, fennel wine. It was good for the eyes, for the stimulation of sexual urges, stopping of nausea, relieving of pleurisy, and avoidance of dropsy and leprosy[2] – a useful panacea in any household. Arnald's recipe for a cough medicine made from wine suggests his methods:

> Wine for a cough and huskiness and asthma is made by having the power of anise, fennel, and licorice added to wine, in such a way that the licorice be twice as much as the others. This you shall drink continuously for it is pleasant and reliable.[3]

However, not all wine was pleasant or enjoyable. Peter of Blois, the brilliant and sharp-tongued clerk at Henry II's court, described in one of his best-known letters the kind of wine the royal household was often served:

> The wine is turned sour or mouldy: thick, greasy, stale, flat, and smacking of pitch. I have sometimes seen even great lords served with wine so muddy that a man must needs close his eyes and clench his teeth, wry-mouthed and shuddering, and filtering the stuff rather than drinking.[4]

Perhaps the king's butlers had some excuse since such a large amount of wine had to be bought and kept in reasonably good condition to satisfy the needs of the court. Even the magnates found it hard to arrange their purchases of wine. Grosseteste suggested to the countess of Lincoln that she should plan to make her major purchases of wine at the fair at Boston, at Southampton, and at Bristol. If she divided her purchases in this way, she could allot enough to each location to stock her nearby manors.[1] The bishop does not mention the practical point which was undoubtedly present in his mind, that this foresight would also prove economical as it would shorten the distances for inland transport and cut the carriage charges. Those responsible for taking the king's wines worked on much the same principle, and wine was distributed from the main ports and great fairs to the various royal residences. The amounts required are startlingly large. At Boston fair alone, the king regularly took two hundred tuns of wine, and had them carted to his nearby establishments;[2] even this quantity was only a small part of a yearly supply.

Unfortunately, it is impossible to form a clear impression of the actual consumption of wine during the thirteenth century since the precise information is lacking; but a contemporary list of the supplies needed to maintain a full wartime guard of one thousand men at Dover castle sets the wine required at one quart a day per person.[3] This was probably a minimum allowance, suitable for a period of siege, but it does suggest the nature of daily consumption.

Not all the wine purchased by a great household was used only for its own needs. Gifts of wine were frequent, and gratefully received; the amounts were determined by the status and wealth of the giver, as well as by his friendliness for the recipient. Where the king might send a tun of wine to one of his favourites, the countess of Leicester would order the dispatch of a sester or two to friends; these might be religious, or important personages such as the messengers of the king of France.[4] Frequently a departing guest was sent on his way with wine for his journey.[5]

The ordinary members of the household enjoyed their ale

6. Military provision cart carrying helmets and hauberks as well as
food and cooking pots

From the *Maciejowski Bible*, M639 f.27v

7a. David and Bathsheba
From the *Maciejowski Bible*, M638 f.41v

7b. Huntsmen pursuing a stag with greyhounds and other dogs
From the *Book of King Modus*, M820 f.12

as much as their superiors their wine. Even earlier than the thirteenth century ale was recognized as the pre-eminent English drink. William Fitzstephen, describing Becket's triumphant journey through France, emphasized the barrels of ale which the chancellor took with him: "decocted from choice fat grain . . . a drink most wholesome, clear of all dregs, rivalling wine in colour and surpassing it in savour".[1] Gerald of Wales, who disapproved so readily of the monks, was particularly shocked by a monastic feast at Canterbury because the table was so loaded with clarry, must, and mead "that beer, such as is made at its best in England, and above all in Kent, found no place among them. There beer among other drinks is as potherbs among made dishes."[2] But all this twelfth-century enthusiasm for healthy ale does not give any useful information as to how it was made. Despite Gerald's reference to Kent it seems certain that hops were not used for brewing as early as the thirteenth century, at any rate in England. Ale was made from barley, and wheat or oats, or even from a mixture of all three.

The price of ale was as strictly controlled as that of bread, because it was a basic commodity for the great mass of the population. The Assize of Ale was worked out on the same sliding scale as the Assize of Bread, that is, the price of ale varied in ratio to the price of grain. However there were a few extra complications:

When the quarter of wheat is worth from 3s to 40d and of barley from 20d to 2s and of oats 16d, then two gallons of ale should be sold for a penny within cities, and outside them it should be three gallons for a penny. But when three gallons are sold for a penny in a borough, then four gallons should be sold for a penny in country towns. Furthermore, when a quarter of barley is sold for 2s, then four gallons should be sold for a penny. . . . And in this way the rate can be raised or lowered according to the market price of corn.[3]

With such confusing regulations, it is not surprising to find that enforcing price control was not easy in the thirteenth century either. The manorial accounts, which include the income from the manor courts, are filled with a constant series of fines levied for breaking the Assize of Ale, as well as that of Bread.

The control of brewing was primarily in the hands of women or of monastic houses, and it was usually the ale-wives who figured among the breakers of the Assize of Ale. In fact this was so much taken for granted that Cesarius of Heisterbach, the thirteenth-century German Cistercian, included the story of an honest ale-wife among his miracles. This poor widow who brewed and sold ale for a livelihood had her house threatened by fire. In desperation she lined up all her measuring pots, as the flames licked at the door, and prayed that if she had ever given false measure her house might be burnt; otherwise she begged that God should spare her and her furniture. The fire stopped short at her measures, and Cesarius, thunderstruck, acclaimed it as an obvious, and unexpected, miracle.[1]

The countess's household was sufficiently large and self-contained for it to normally take care of its requirements for ale by brewing from its own stores of grain. During the winter, the countess had a special ale-wife from Banbury, a town particularly renowned for its brewing, whose wages were 5s, and who was also paid 18d for her expenses home from Odiham.[2] In May a debt was settled with Lady Wimarc of Odiham for several quarters of malted grains bought when the countess first returned to Odiham.[3] Normally, however, brewing was part of the standard routine of the household, with extra purchases made whenever there was a sudden demand. When the household moved to Dover the problem became more difficult. At the beginning of July 10½ quarters of barley were brewed at the Maison Dieu in Dover. The grain was taken from the castle stores, and the countess paid 10d for the milling and 3s 1d for the necessary firewood. After the brewing was completed, the draff – the usual perquisite of the brewer – was left at the Maison Dieu.[1]

Later in the summer ale was more frequently bought than brewed, and during the last days of the account there was no ale at all. Because it was such a basic commodity the price was very low and the quantities very great. In the countess's account, the price of ale varied from a halfpenny to three farthings a gallon, and two hundred gallons or more were bought at a time. Roger Leyburn, with his small travelling household, bought sixty-five gallons at a time, also at an average cost of three farthings.[2] Although the amount of grain used in brewing is carefully specified, there is no easy method of discovering how much ale a given quantity of grain was supposed to make, despite the sliding scale set up by the Assize of Ale.

A great baronial household normally had a very generous allowance of ale. Many peasants would not be so fortunate, so that in some of the contemporary manorial custumaries any special allowance would be carefully described. One such example, from the beginning of the fourteenth century, tells how the hundredman at Christmas was allowed to have as much good ale as he liked to drink "as long as the daylight lasts". In addition after dark all the tenants were to have more fire-wood and two candles so that they could sit and drink as long as the two candles, burning one after the other, should last.[3] The manorial tenants' Christmas feast was a poor affair compared to the elegant dinner in the hall of a great castle, but at all levels wine or ale to an overwhelming degree made the feast.

7

Cooking and Serving of Meals

The contemporary household rolls can tell us what ingredients were at the cook's disposal, but not of course how they were cooked or served. Some information on these matters can be gleaned from other sources, but unfortunately the two most complete guides to medieval cookery, *The Forme of Cury** and *The Goodman of Paris*† were written at the end of the fourteenth century and for households which differed sharply from the baronial household of the thirteenth century. The diet of the fourteenth century was more varied than that of the thirteenth, for a greater number of vegetables and spices had come into common use. All the same both works are useful guides to the ingredients and methods of preparation of those thirteenth-century dishes whose names are known, for recipes changed little from generation to generation.

We are also fortunate in having a vivid picture, in the Luttrell Psalter, of the actual appearance of a medieval kitchen and serving pantry. The illustrator was fascinated by the humble details of everyday life and produced a series of charming vignettes picturing the ordinary occupations of the household. On two facing pages he depicts the duties of the chief cook and his many assistants, while the following

* *The Forme of Cury*, the first English cookery book, was a collection of recipes made by the royal cooks of Richard II.

† *The Goodman of Paris*, one of the most charming treatises of the Middle Ages, was written by a bourgeois of Paris, c. 1393, as a manual of instruction for his young wife. It is most comprehensive including moral tales, menus and markets, the diseases of horses, falconry, as well as recipes and household hints.

leaves show how the prepared dishes were handed over to the carver and the servers for their ceremonious presentation to the high table.[1] Certain details betray that this was a household of the fourteenth century, but the picture of the kitchen, and the illustration of the whole manner of cooking and service, belong to a long period of medieval life. The illuminator's work gives an extraordinarily clear idea of the means and methods by which a baronial household was served.

The necessary equipment in the medieval kitchen was meagre. Meat to be roasted was put on a spit directly over the fire, and usually turned by hand. Boiling was a far more common method of cooking meat, and pots of all sizes were essential. By the thirteenth century earthenware cooking utensils were being replaced by metal ones, but both materials were used for the characteristic pots of the period. There was the great round-bottomed cauldron, a pot closely resembling the one pictured in the Bayeux Tapestry that was quite possibly directly descended from the Roman pot. The cauldron was hung over the fire by a hook and chain designed with teeth so that the pot could be easily raised or lowered as the heat of the fire or the speed of the cooking demanded. The other characteristic type of pot, which was even more common than the cauldron, had three short legs and little handles at either side of the neck. It too could be suspended by a chain, but it was also capable of standing directly in the flames. This style of pot appeared in many sizes, all roughly designed for hard wear.

Apart from his pots, the cook had certain necessary implements. The Luttrell Psalter emphasized the mortar, with a truly enormous pestle, but an iron flesh-hook must have been the tool in most constant use. This was a long fork-like affair with a wooden handle, but with its two or three prongs attached to the side rather than to the end. The prongs were somewhat hooked to aid in pulling large joints of meat out of the massive cauldrons. The cook in the

Luttrell Psalter also had a long, slotted spoon, rather like a long-handled colander, with which he stirred the contents of his pots. Large knives, and a cleaver with which to cut up carcasses, were the other essentials.

Since the countess of Leicester's cook had to feed the large numbers of her household, as well as frequent guests, under primitive and changing conditions he must often have found his work heavy. Certainly a good cook was invaluable; Adam Marsh thought it a striking sign of the countess's regard for Bishop Grosseteste that she was willing to lend him hers.[1] The duties of this important servant are very variously described; John of Garland insists exclusively on the washing up, and the author of *Fleta* mentions only the obligation to account for the number of dishes he served.[2] The recipes prove that the cook's talent for cooking was important, although the *Forme of Cury* suggests that a strong right arm was an indispensable preliminary: practically all its recipes for meat, poultry, and fish begin with the sturdy admonition to "Smite hem to pecys".

Not all dishes required great skill, for they could be as simple as dried beans boiled in broth and eaten with bacon.[3] Such a dish would be the major item in the diet of the poor, usually without the bacon, and may well have served as a side dish in the Leicester household for there are many references to beans in the accounts. The countess's cook might prefer to serve the ubiquitous bean in a slightly more elegant form, in which case it could be cooked with onions and coloured with saffron.[4] Few of the surviving recipes are so simple. The medieval baron liked a complicated and highly seasoned dish, such as soles served with a sauce of boiled onions, saffron and honey clarified with salt.[5] Plaice called for a sauce of bread, broth and vinegar, seasoned with ginger, salt, pepper and cinnamon.[6] Meats were also served with highly spiced sauces. In the Goodman's garnished brewet – a kind of thin stew – the sauce was made with ginger, cinnamon, pepper, saffron, cloves and grain of Paradise, as well as onions, parsley, wine, verjuice, and vinegar.[1] The use of rice and almonds in very large quantities must have been one of the few bland elements in such a highly seasoned diet.

Although it is tempting to continue detailing the various recipes which strike the imagination by their remoteness from the less exotic diet of today, it must be remembered that the basic requirements of the good cook have not varied much from Chaucer's specifications:

> To boille the chiknes with the marybones,
> And poudre-marchant tart and galyngale,
> Wel koude he know a draughte of Londonn ale,
> He koude roste, and sethe, and broille, and frye,
> Maken mortreux, and wel bake a pye.

The difficulty of obtaining a good cook is also perennial. Robert Mannyng noted that rich men are never satisfied with their cook, even though every cook wishes his meat was well served.[2] Frequently the cooks of the wealthy and important were short-tempered and overbearing; their tempers were more noticeable, and more easily provoked under the peripatetic conditions of medieval life. The cook of a great lord, or bishop, might find himself at work in conditions which changed from day to day, depending on the particular places that his lord visited. Under such circumstances, their bad tempers are certainly under-standable. Jacques de Vitry tells the story of a bishop's cook who was so exacting that he finally drove his temporary host to sacrilege. When the bishop was on visitation, his cook demanded innumerable dishes to be prepared for his master's use. The host cleric was finally exhausted by the cook's importunities, and exclaimed in despair: "I have nothing more to give except the flanks of the Crucifix", which he had roasted and put on the bishop's table.[3]

The nature of cooks may be changeless, the pattern of meals varies from age to age. In the Middle Ages it was usual to have two meals a day; the main one, a very large and formal dinner in the forenoon; the other, a much lighter supper where more emphasis was placed on drink than on substantial food. The hours of these meals fluctuated according to the season, since the household's working day ran from sunrise to sunset. Dinner was served at about the fifth of the twelve daylight hours, roughly between ten and eleven in the morning. Supper came after the day's work was over and when the light was waning, between about four and six. Breakfast was not a formal meal for which the household gathered, but consisted of a snack of bread and ale or watered wine taken after mass. The writers on manners suggest that a more substantial breakfast was a concession to children and the sick, or to ladies who were overly pale or troubled with bad breath. One such writer advised that "good wine colours the face, and anise, fennel, and cinnamon correct the other".[1] Rere suppers, an extra supper after the ordinary evening meal, were especially condemned by the moralists as leading to gluttony and lechery. Robert Mannyng draws a disapproving picture of the rere suppers indulged in by the squires and servitors of the knights. All day they had been sober before their masters, but once their lords were gone to bed, then they caroused past midnight and on to cockcrow.[2] The moralists also deplored dinners set so early on Sunday that they were begun before the high mass was completed. Robert Mannyng even found it necessary to inveigh against the gluttonous priest who was willing to leave the altar with his mass unfinished to go to dinner.[3]

Dinner was not only the main meal but also the great social occasion of the day. Grosseteste in his *Rules* devoted considerable attention to the importance of the proper service and placing of guests, and also the supervision of the hall by the lord or lady of the house.[4] From her account it is clear that Eleanor observed the bishop's rule of eating with her household, for the clerk carefully recorded her presence each day before that of any of her guests. There were only two occasions when she was absent from the hall; a brief trip in April, and the days in August when she mourned her husband and son after the tragic news from Evesham.[1]

The established order of preparing the hall and the company for dinner was generally understood and practised. Bartholomew the Englishman put into words the details often pictured in the manuscript illuminations:

At feasts, first meat is prepared and arrayed, guests be called together, forms and stools be set in the hall, and tables, cloths, and towels be ordained, disposed and made ready. Guests be set with the lord in the chief place of the board, and they sit not down at the board before the guests wash their hands. Children be set in their place, and servants at a table by themselves. First knives, spoons, and salts be set on the board, and then bread and drink, and many divers messes. Household servants busily help each other to do everything diligently, and talk merrily together. The guests are gladded with lutes and harps. Now wine and messes of meat are brought forth and departed. At the last cometh fruit and spices, and when they have eaten, cloths and relief [trestles] are borne away, and guests wash and wipe their hands again. The grace is said, and guests thank the lord. Then, for gladness and comfort, drink is brought yet again.[2]

This, in a rather more polished style and in greater detail, is the same procedure recommended by Grosseteste in his regulations for the service of dinner in hall.

Enough of the objects used in this formal service have survived to make it possible to visualize the great hall at dinner time. The ewers, which held the water with which the guests washed their hands both before and after meals, were among the most handsome of the household goods. Often they show the lively imagination of their maker, and the pottery or bronze ewer might have a figure, such as a woman or a ram's head, as a handle. Frequently the ewer, or aquamanile as it was sometimes called, was made in the shape of a knight on horseback, and when tilted the water poured from the horse's mouth. Bowls were used to catch the water, and ranged from inexpensive earthenware to carved bronze.

There are also examples of the types of knives and spoons used. Plenty of silver spoons seems to have been one of the common marks of wealth. Two dozen silver spoons were made for the king's children at Windsor in 1254, at a total cost of 27s 8d.[1] Even an ordinary citizen of London might leave as many as three dozen spoons, as illustrated by a will of 1290.[2] Other wills of the same period go into further detail. Thus, the Master of Sherborne Hospital left a dozen silver spoons to Osbert of Bridport, while the others were to be given to the Master's chaplains, clerks, squires, special serjeants and domestics.[3] The length of the list of possible heirs suggests a rather large number of spoons. Silver spoons were carefully repaired after they had been in service for some time; one of the first general entries on the countess's roll accounts for eight silver pennies, used to mend four broken spoons.[4]

Each person had his own knife, which he carried when not in use in a sheath hung from his girdle. These sheaths were of leather, normally decorated with semi-heraldic designs, and were very cheap; those made for the countess only cost 2d.[5] The knives themselves were mainly of the ancient type known as scramasax and remained much the same during the whole period, so that only an archaeologist can date them with any precision.

One of the prides of the wealthy household was its supply of plate. The thirteenth-century baron did not normally have the highly ornamented salts which became such a notable feature of the later medieval table. Generally the wealth of his household was displayed in the number of his cups, salts, and platters of precious materials. Very few examples survive, because plate was subject to many changes. It might, for example, be melted down when its owner ran short of money; often it was refashioned to suit the changed tastes in decoration of another generation. Thus Bogo de

Clare had four dishes and four silver saucers made new from four old dishes and five saucers, and the re-working cost 18s 6d.[1] It is hard to ascertain the proportion between the intrinsic value of the metal and the cost of the workmanship; but a gilded plate, weighing 17d* and costing 2s 10d, bought by the countess of Leicester for her daughter, suggests that it was about half and half.[2]

Cups are the most frequently described of all plate and often appear in accounts and wills. Early in Henry III's reign, when relations between the king and Simon de Montfort were friendly, the queen had given the earl two silver cups weighing more than 5 marks.[3] Bogo de Clare's account mentions nine valuable cups bought, ranging in price from 20s to £7, a clear indication of his wealth.[4] The Master of Sherborne Hospital provides a less luxurious example in his will. His sister was to have his drinking horn set in silver; his niece a cup of Indian nut – coconut, perhaps? – with its foot and setting of silver; Lord John Gylet, a cup of crystal with a silver foot. Other less valuable silver cups and five old silver platters and salts were to be melted and made into chalices for church use.[5] Glass cups appeared on the account of young Henry, and two were bought for him and his sister in 1273 for the modest price of 5d.[6]

Another type of cup at this time was the mazer. Mazers were shallow bowls of maple wood, usually finished with a silver rim, sometimes with a silver foot and cover. They were the very best kind of wooden cups, and were so valuable that even such an important man as the bishop of Hereford had his mazer carefully repaired at a cost of 10d.[7] Naturally they were particularly prized possessions in middle-class families. In 1282 a widow at Oxford left her daughter her most cherished belongings, including a mazer cup with foot, as well as several brass pots and pitchers, hangings and sheets. Her niece received the mazer cup without a foot, one silver spoon, and a small pillow as her second-best share.[8]

* I.e. the weight of seventeen silver pennies.

These mazer cups were thus of second rank; not as valuable as the silver, but finer and more permanent than the common wooden and earthenware cups.

We can picture the tables spread for dinner. At the high table the silver plate, cups, and spoons of the household were proudly displayed. Each two persons shared a dish, the young serving the older, or the man the lady; they transferred their helpings to their own trencher or manchet, a thick piece of day-old bread. In well-run households these pieces of gravy-soaked bread were gathered up after the meal and distributed to the poor, along with any remaining scraps. Bishop Grosseteste emphasized the need of the ranking figure at the high table having a well-filled plate, so that he could share the bits from his own dish with others as a polite mark of particular favour.[1] Dishes, platters, and cups, made of earthenware or fine-grained wood, were cheap, and were used for the less important members of the household. The accounts illustrate how frequently and inexpensively such supplies could be bought. The countess of Leicester purchased one thousand dishes for 6s 8d when she was awaiting the arrival of Earl Simon and his retinue.[2] Roger Leyburn twice bought fifty cups, within a short space of time, and paid only between a farthing and a half-penny each.[3] King Henry himself found it necessary to acquire one thousand wine pitchers at Kingston for use at the great feast of St Edward; for the reasonable price of 21s 6d they were even carried to Westminster and delivered to the king's butler.[4]

The illuminations illustrate the procession which converged on the hall to serve the dinner once the table was set. The butler was responsible for serving the wine and the beer, and a young squire would serve the lord and lady their cup and carve their meat. Everyone was supposed to be pleasant and gay. Indeed Bartholomew the Englishman devoted a special section to the need of the lord of the house to be cheerful, for he says "the supper is not worthy to be praised if the lord of the house be melancholy."[5]

The practice of the time was to serve a large number of dishes in each course. The Goodman of Paris, giving some sample menus for his young wife, described meat dinners of six courses, with twenty-four or thirty different dishes. Fish dinners were more restrained, as befitted Lent or fast days; they averaged only three courses, but again with many separate dishes.[1] All the courses repeated the same kinds of food until the very last – sometimes called the issue – which presented fruits, nuts, and sweetmeats. No necessary division or progression can be observed in the massive servings brought first to the high table by the procession of servitors, and then distributed among the less important.

In his vocabulary, Walter of Bibblesworth* described a magnificent feast. It commenced with a boar's head garlanded with banners and flowers, and continued with venison, frumenty, cranes, peacocks, swans, kids, suckling pigs, pheasants, partridges, larks, woodcock and plover. The final touch of elegance was to have the little birds powdered with rose sugar.[2] The suspicion arises that Walter, like earlier compilers of vocabularies, was trying to include in one feast all the foods he had ever heard of, combined in a single splendid orgy. Certainly these elegant dishes were not the usual fare of a baronial household. There was plenty of beef, mutton, pork and poultry, but none of the delicacies of which Walter wrote with such feeling – only "the great and common meat, as it is used at dinner".[3]

What constituted a feast depended greatly on the nature of the ordinary fare. Gerald of Wales, at Canterbury, was as shocked by the number of the monks' dishes as by the variety of their drinks. He mentioned with disapproval that there were sixteen or more,[4] although it must be allowed

---

* Walter of Bibblesworth wrote his vocabulary at the end of the thirteenth century to teach French to the children of the English barons. As a man of good family his work shows the particular interests of the baronial class, and is also far more rural in character than that of John of Garland.

that they were all fish dishes, for the Benedictines had not yet come to the relaxation of the rule against meat. Much simpler was the feast, described by Salimbene in enthusiastic detail, which the Franciscans at Sens gave to Louis IX when he passed through their town. The friars had fresh cherries, white bread, fresh beans cooked with milk, fish and eel pies – rich with almond milk and cinnamon – roasted eel with "the best sauce", and fruits, along with an abundance of wine.[1] This was frugal compared to the dishes itemized by the secular writers, but certainly, from the tone of Salimbene's comments, a far cry from their usual meagre dinner.

In contrast to dinner, supper was a more informal and enjoyable meal, described by the writers as lighter and more intimate. Bishop Grosseteste, for example, recommended only a few light dishes and cheese at supper.[2] Bartholomew the Englishman, always rather long-winded, went into great detail in his description of supper. Perhaps this was because he hit on the happy idea of comparing it with the Old Testament feast of Ahasuerus, and so could work through all the possible points of comparison. His emphasis on the need for light, from candles or torches, was singularly practical: "For it is shame to sup in darkness and perilous also for flies and other filth." But Brother Bartholomew was particularly impressed by the deliciousness of the meats served for supper, and the fact that it went on so long: "For men use, after full end of work and of travel to sit long at supper. For meat eaten too hastily is harmful when the night comes. Therefore, at the supper, men should eat by leisure and not too hastily."[3] Yet he does not suggest that his contemporaries should attempt to copy the length of Ahasuerus's feast – it went on one hundred and fifty days!

The literary discussion of the proper methods of serving and the formal ritual of meals was complemented by the equally stringent etiquette prescribed for the diners. The manual of manners was a very popular form during the Middle Ages, which enjoyed all types of didactic literature.

Probably the most comprehensive contemporary treatise on table manners is that of Fra Bonvesin dell Riva.* Some of his precepts belong to the basic code of courtesy which parents still struggle to implant in their young. Don't talk with your mouth full, don't use the table as a prop, don't suck from your spoon, don't start fights at table; all these injunctions have a timeless ring. However, many of the friar's courtesies belong to purely medieval conditions, when forks were unusual, a dish was meant to serve two in common, and the wine cup was passed from person to person. It was, for example, proper to hold the great cup by only one hand, and that usually under the bowl, when passing it to another, the gesture so commonly seen in pictures of great feasts. Yet the friar exhorted his readers to hold the cup with both hands when they themselves were drinking, and to be sure to wipe their mouths well. All the friar's advice has a strictly practical tone, although his standard of service made allowance for the common frailties of both servers and cooks. He adjured the servers to be sure and keep their thumbs on the rims of the dishes, but suggested to the guests that they should refrain from mentioning any fly or dirt they saw in the food. Given the exposed nature of the medieval kitchen and the distances the food was carried to the table, these mischances must have been quite common. But the friar considered the interest of the guests, too; one of his last suggestions was to warn a diner that he should not put his knife back in its sheath too soon, as there might be something else coming he would want to eat.[1]

Meals were occasionally taken away from home. We have already seen how the countess of Leicester bought dinner on the road for her household.[2] The more common practice, since a large household on the move was always accompanied

* Bonvesin dell Riva was an Italian friar, a member of the order of the Umiliati. He taught in Milan, and not only wrote the *Fifty Courtesies of the Table* c. 1290, but was also the author of an enthusiastic description of the wonders of the city of Milan.

by a long string of carts, was for the cook to provide dinner on a picnic basis. The account of Bishop Swinfield shows that it was even possible for the travelling cook to hire his kitchen utensils for the day.[1] Even at such casual meals the formality of spreading the cloth was carefully observed. One delightful contemporary manuscript illumination shows Ruth eating with the gleaners in the fields of Boaz. The cloth has been carefully spread over the knees of all those sitting down, and a jug of wine or beer supports the bowl.[2]

Outdoor meals appealed especially to lovers for the privacy they gave. In the romance of *Jehan et Blonde*, the young man and his lady-love escaped together but, even in their haste, they stopped for a picnic under the branches. Jehan's faithful servant found them white bread and pasties of capon, washed down by wine from the two barrels that the provident Jehan always carried. They spread a well-embroidered towel on the green lawn for their tablecloth, and dined happily while their horses cropped the grass.[3] The romance gives a rather glamorous description of a common practice.

Whether the meal was served inside or out, the illuminating sidelights cast by the contemporary authors and artists add life and colour to the bare entries of the account. They help us to form a coherent picture of the accepted pattern of meals and service in a great baronial household.

8

Cloths and Clothes

The men and women of the Middle Ages loved bright and luxurious clothes; they were among the major items of expenditure. A look at the manuscript illuminations shows the love of colour by both sexes: bright gowns, brilliant mantles, and gaudy stockings, all stand out against the dark walls.* The household account, which always included the expenditure on materials to be used for clothes, gives useful information on the kinds of cloth, fur and ornaments bought, though we depend on other sources to tell us how they were made.

The countess of Leicester's account is no exception to the general rule, although the items in it which deal with clothes are somewhat affected by the unusual circumstances of the time. Thomas Wykes, the vigorously pro-royalist chronicler, wrote with disgust of the rise of prices during the period of Simon de Montfort's rule, because of the interference with foreign trade. The chronicler mentioned, with particular disdain, that many took to wearing undyed cloths to please the earl of Leicester, thus proclaiming that they had heeded Simon's request to refrain from foreign trade.[1] If Adam

* The actual brightness of the colours of cloth is, of course, impossible to prove now. Some of the vegetable dyes, such as woad for blue and weld for yellow, may have tended to be muddy and uneven, especially on cloths which had not been properly prepared for dyeing. However, the reds, such as crimson, vermilion, and "grain", made from the *coccus* insects, and purple, prepared from the liquid secreted by the mollusk *murex*, were certainly brilliant. As today, the wealthier members of society could buy the finest materials, and, in the Middle Ages, this meant those with the brightest colours.

Marsh is to be believed, the Countess Eleanor when younger had all the usual feminine weakness for magnificent clothes. In one of Adam's longest and most didactic letters, he cautioned her specially on the need to watch against excesses in dress.[1] Yet by 1265 the countess was older and more sedate, and burdened with more serious problems. Perhaps for these reasons, as well as the disturbed state of the realm, the items in the account for clothing are almost at a minimum. The entries from other accounts of the time are more illuminating, but deal almost exclusively with men's clothes.

All members of a medieval household, even important officials, were annually provided with robes, and sometimes shoes, as part of their wages; both the amounts in money and the quality of the robes were based on a sliding scale. Since robes were normally given at Christmas, the fragment of the countess's account does not cover the relevant period for her household. However the account of Henry, Edward I's son, gives some idea of the nature of the prevailing scale. Thus the guardian of the king's children, who had the ultimate superintendence of Henry's household, received £30 annually in wages and a robe worth 45s 6d. The clerk in charge of the household's daily affairs had wages of only 4½d a day, but his robe like that of the nurses, was worth 30s 8d – a valuable increment to his salary. The ordinary domestic officials, such as the cook, the pantler, the usher and the tailor, had wages of 2d a day, and their robes were worth only 9s.[2] The difference in social status between the servants and the clerk or the nurses is clearly shown by the value of their clothes.

A common form of present at any level of medieval society was the bestowal of a robe, which in Henry III's time usually included a tunic, super-tunic, and cloak. Such a gift might be made to either men or women, as the basic elements of their dress were much the same, though the cut was not, and the quality of the materials illustrated the recipient's place on the social scale. Thus Alice of Godstow was given a

tunic, super-tunic, a cloak with a hood, and a furred coverlet, all of russet, as well as a coverlet of rabbit-skins, and a
white counterpane of linen.[1] This was a generous gift, but
of cloth and furs worn only by the poor. The robes the king
gave to his friends and relations were far more elegant; part
of the royal Christmas present to Eleanor in 1238 was a
piece of gold baudekin cloth for a robe with a super-tunic,
which was also to be lined and trimmed with miniver.[2]

Those who were not fortunate, or useful, enough to receive
new robes as gifts or as part of their wages might still hope
to be given the cast-off clothes of the great as charity. There
was considerable competition among the greedy for such
welcome largess. The duty of the royal almoner to see that
the king did not give his robes to the minstrels and flatterers
who surrounded him has already been mentioned. Perhaps
the almoner's concern in this matter was having some effect,
as the thirteenth-century minstrels frequently complain of
the niggardliness of their hosts; they felt that a gift of the
lord's old robe was one of the rightful rewards of their
profession. In addition a robe used only on a ceremonial
occasion was often a valuable perquisite for a higher servant.
When Simon de Montfort officiated for the first time as
Steward of England at King Henry's marriage feast in 1236,
he was bound by the tradition of his office to hand over his
robe at the end of the ceremony to the master-cook.[3] Nor
did the Middle Ages share the modern prejudice against old
clothes. A striking feature of the early wills is the number of
legacies of specific articles of apparel, all described in loving
detail. Obviously these tunics and furred mantles were one
of the most valuable parts of the inventory. Few people,
however, went as far as the Oxford widow who carefully
gave her best super-tunic to one person, and then arranged
for the fur from it to be given to the next of her heirs, and
so on down the line.[4]

It is necessary to look at the different materials used for
these various garments before attempting to discover the

main lines of fashion in the mid-thirteenth century. There were three important types of materials in use: wool, silk, and linen. The woollen cloths were used most and in this field England was still supreme. The elegant silks worn only by the rich were imported from France, from the east, but especially from Italy. Finally there were the linens, some imported from France and some made in England. They ranged in quality from the finest type known as "sindon",* which seems to have been a lawn or delicate muslin, to the coarse and ubiquitously useful canvas. Furs, which lined and trimmed the wools and the silks, are a separate matter.

Certain English towns had a special reputation for certain kinds of woollen cloth. The scarlets of Lincoln were the finest of all, and the description had much of the prestige of an accepted brand-name. Incidentally scarlet in the thirteenth century was still a type of cloth, not necessarily a colour, a point which is underlined by two entries in the countess's account, one for red scarlet for Richard of Cornwall, the other for "sanguine" scarlet for the countess herself and her daughter. These scarlets were the most expensive of all woollens, costing the countess 7s an ell.[1] Perse, though much cheaper than scarlet, was normally a fine dark-blue woollen and relatively expensive though the countess purchased 24½ ells† of perse for the servants' robes at a total cost of only 42s.[2] This is so cheap that the perse must have been of particularly poor quality.

Some of the other varieties of the English cloth market are both hard to define and trace. The halbergetts of Stamford puzzle even the most eminent scholar in the field.[3] There is also a running debate as to whether the "stamforts",

* The actual nature of sindon is still a matter of dispute among scholars. There is no general agreement on whether it was a very fine linen or a silk, but I have followed the interpretation preferred by the editors of the Liberate Rolls.

† The ell was the most frequent measure of length for cloth. It varied in different countries, but in England it was commonly 45 inches.

so frequently mentioned on the Continent at this time, were in fact cloth from Stamford or just a heavy type of worsted derived from the term *stamen forte*. Beverley was the place for burnets, a common material for hose, but King Henry also bought burnets from Northampton.[1] Russets and burels were normally the coarsest and cheapest cloths of all, used mainly by the poor and distributed as alms. They were made almost everywhere, but the russets of Colchester had gained a special reputation. The Countess Eleanor had worn russet during the early days of her first widowhood, and after Evesham she turned to it again. The roll records the large purchase of 34 ells in London, at the extraordinarily high price of 112s 4d – over 3s an ell.[2] The price is probably to be explained by an unusually fine quality. Ten ells of black serge for only 17s were bought for Richard de Montfort before his departure for Bigorre; this quantity was sufficient for a robe and also trappings for his horse.[3]

The very coarse woollen cloths, such as chalons or blanchet, were meant primarily for bed-coverings, or for heavy outside wear. Chalons were named after the French town of Châlons-sur-Marne, but they had also been made in England for many years. Winchester and Guildford seem to have been centres of their manufacture, and a Winchester custumary of the thirteenth century carefully set their size as well as the amount to be paid by each loom. The heavy rug-like cloth was used as a coverlet or counterpane, and was made in three standard sizes; four ells by two yards, three and a half yards by one and three quarters, or three ells by one and a half ells.[4] The countess bought blanchet for the chamber, while Bishop Swinfield equipped the friar in charge of supervising the manors with the same cloth,[5] but no convenient custumary explains its nature. We only know that it was heavy and considered fit only for the roughest use.

The silks were imported and expensive, so it is not surprising that they are not represented in the countess's account, nor in the moderate expenditures of the bishop of Hereford. Such items as baudekin and samite were rare and expensive even in peaceful times. Primarily used for religious vestments and church hangings, they figured also as special luxuries among the clothes of the wealthy and the great. In 1256 King Henry paid Luke de Lucca* £6 for three gold-wrought baudekins, and £4 for a piece of saffron samite.[1] Although the Countess Eleanor also purchased some of her cloths from the same merchant, she bought far more modestly than her brother. Her purchases were not of silk, but of scarlet and lawn, and, even at that, she was not able to settle all her debt, for she owed Luke 42s.[2] These merchants of Lucca represented the very flourishing silk industry of their city during the thirteenth century. The Luccan weavers could imitate all the Oriental stuffs, and their products were to be found at the fairs of Champagne, as well as at the merchants of Paris or London. After 1300 the balance of success and prosperity tipped towards the silk weavers of Florence, but in the middle of the century the merchant from Lucca was the most highly regarded in London.

The unfamiliar terms used for the various silks are indeed confusing, and seem to have perplexed even the contemporary clerks for they were very variously described. A brief explanation of the most commonly accepted kinds may illuminate the matter a little. Baudekin for example derived its name from Bagdad, where it was made, and it was well known in both France and England. It was often brocaded with gold, and generally decorated with figures. Samite, also a costly silk, was of Greek origin, though the Arabs and the Cypriots later learned the secret of its manufacture. Sendal was a type of taffeta, which could vary greatly in quality

* Luke de Lucca was the leading thirteenth-century Italian merchant in London. Henry III made many of his most extensive purchases of cloth from him, while on the accession of Edward, Luke came to occupy a commanding position as "king's merchant" until his death in 1279.

and was much used for banners, and even for tents. Damask, called after Damascus where it was made, is the only one of these names that looks really familiar to modern eyes. It meant then, as now, a heavy stuff with designs woven in the body of the material.[1]

Although the countess mentions the purchase of "rayed", or striped, cloths for her brother Richard and his son,[2] it is not clear whether these were woollen or silk cloths; probably they were wool. The rayed cloth dyed "in the grain", that is with the finest dye known as grain, was of about the same value as scarlet, costing 8s the ell but imported from Paris. However rayed cloth was not necessarily fine. A quantity was also used to pay John La Warre's archers and provide a robe for the barber;[3] it must have been of poor quality as it cost only 1s 7d an ell. Despite its cheapness, so much was needed for the twenty-nine archers that the countess was unable to pay the merchant from whom she made the purchase.

Camlet was another imported cloth, with a long nap like plush, woven from camel's hair or goat's hair, especially the very fine goat's hair of Asia Minor. The great majority of these camlets came from Cyprus, and they were frequently used for winter robes, like those King Henry had purchased in 1254 to be made up for his children at Windsor.[4] The entry on the roll draws attention to a peculiarity of this cloth, and indeed of most of the woollen cloths: they were bought with the nap very long, and had to be shorn before they were made up. Both Bishop Swinfield's and Bogo de Clare's accounts show that this practice was a regular expense included in the purchase of cloth. The cost of shearing seems to have averaged about 1s a cloth.[5] In fact, when woollen clothes became dirty and worn, they were then re-shorn and a fresh surface exposed. This was a skilled procedure carried out by the merchants who sold cloth, and the countess's account suggests that it was a fairly expensive process. Her chief tailor went twice to London on this errand, and, on one occasion, it cost 12d to shear the countess's robe of perse plus the tailor's expenses of 2s.[1]

The last of the basic materials was linen, which was easily obtained and in common use, although its quality varied enormously. Its use for clothing was mainly restricted to head-coverings and underwear, but linen also served many household needs. Sheets were in general use among the well-to-do, and their fineness reflected the social standing and wealth of the individual. Pillow-slips too were well-known, but sometimes in short supply. Jacques de Vitry tells the story of the monk who had never seen a pillow before entering the monastery but afterwards, when he was lacking a bolster for one night, "because the linen cloth which covered the bolster was being washed", disturbed everyone with his complaining and murmuring.[2] Some of the linen was very rough, and justifiably referred to as canvas. Thus in young Henry's household 12 ells of canvas were bought for "covering saddles, robes, and harness; for napkins; and for cleaning silver platters and other necessaries".[3] This sounds rather hard on the guests, unless the napkins were meant for kitchen use. In the middle of the century the price of linen varied between 3d and 3½d a yard for the poorer quality, and 5d a yard for the better. Bogo de Clare's account describes rather carefully the different kinds of linen and their uses. The finest linen for the lord cost 8d or 9d the ell, while canvas was only 2d. It took 30 ells for a pair of sheets, and 9 ells for a cloth for the table. Towels for the wardrobe were of much finer quality than those for the pantry, and canvas was used for polishing the silver and for kitchen needs.[4]

The practice of most households was to buy a large amount of linen cloth at one time and then make it up as it was needed. In the inventory of Cecily Huse, who died in 1267, thirty-nine ells of linen were listed, as well as three cloths and five towels. Cecily had mentioned in her will that she wanted all the cloths and towels "which are now made or to be made" to be divided among her husband and daughters.[1] The countess of Leicester bought fifty-four ells of canvas in July, for a little less than 3d a yard, and two pairs of towels for the chamber, at a cost of 2s 8d;[2] but her expenses for linen were really very small.

The duties of the laundress must have included the washing of the large amounts of table linen, as well as the linen clothes. Since the re-shearing of woollen cloths served as a primitive form of dry-cleaning for the outer garments, there was a reasonable emphasis on the need for, and the comfort of, clean clothes. The Goodman of Paris sums up the general attitude of the well-to-do of the time when he enjoined his young wife to see that her husband, on his return home, had his feet washed; and was comforted with clean linen, as well as fresh shoes and hose.[3]

Whether the robes and mantles were of wool or silk, they were almost invariably trimmed, and sometimes lined, with fur, almost a necessity in unheated houses and damp stone castles. There was a considerable range of furs available and most of them sound familiar to modern ears, though an exception must be made for the fur included in a list of the goods traded at Narbonne in the thirteenth century – it was described as "cloaks of dormouse".[4] Generally speaking with fur as with materials, the type worn was determined by the social class of the wearer: kings wore ermine for great occasions; nobles and men of importance wore squirrel – either plain or in a special pattern of dark and light known as vair; ordinary men or women wore byse (probably deerskin), rabbit, or sheepskin.

The detailed listing in Bogo de Clare's account of the robes and furs for all the members of his household shows clearly the social distinctions in dress. The standard amount of cloth required for a robe was apparently seven ells. Each of the ordinary members of the household had striped burnet for cloth, with one fur, and a hood of "budge", or sheepskin. The doctor had a robe of bluet with a squirrel fur, and a hood of "strell", a fur as yet unidentified. Bogo himself had robes of considerable magnificence for a cleric, even if he was the younger brother of the great earl of the Gloucester. The fashionable clerk had a robe and tabard of perse, a robe, tabard, and cloak of scarlet, with five and a half furs, a robe and cloak of linsey-woolsey, and a robe of triple worsted. In addition Bogo had four ells of burnet for hose, and a tunic of "cange", a light material probably like taffeta.[1] After such splendid robes, the cloth ordered by the bishop of Hereford seems very plain indeed. Bishop Swinfield bought coarse "keyneth", bluet and plain linen for himself and his household, and basset for the horse cloths.[2] Swinfield, although a bishop, was neither as important nor as rich as Bogo de Clare. There are only three brief mentions of fur on the countess of Leicester's household account. These include a squirrel fur, at 3s 3d, and two purchases of expensive miniver for young Eleanor and her cousin Edmund.[3]

The social distinctions implied by these different materials and furs were jealously guarded. Indeed Gerald of Wales mentions complacently, as an outstanding proof of his charity and humility, that when his heart was touched by the appeals of the poor he gave away all his furred cloaks that were lined with vair, and after that wore only lambskin.[4] King Louis IX, though with less self-congratulation, refused to wear fine cloths and expensive furs after his return from his first crusade; according to Joinville, he put aside ermine and miniver and scarlet for perse and the cheapest furs.[5] This was such unusual behaviour in a king that it was frequently commented on as a visible sign of mortification, and reinforced the general belief in the king's sanctity.

Such were the basic materials and allowances for the clothes, but it is interesting to try to discover the styles and the manner in which they were combined. Here the accounts, of course, are silent, and it is necessary to turn to the information given by contemporary pictures and carvings, summarized by the historians of costume. Certain main lines are easy to trace. Both men and women wore the same outside garments: tunic, super-tunic, and mantle, although the women's were invariably longer. In fact, in most of the illustrations of the period, it is impossible to see the feet of a fashionable lady at all, as they are covered by her robe. By the middle of the thirteenth century, it had become the style to make these main parts of the costume of the same cloth, and to trim or line the super-tunic, as well as the mantle, with fur.

The tunic, a loose garment like an elongated shirt with long sleeves, slipped over the head, and was slit for convenience at the neck. This slit was properly closed by a brooch, of which the wealth and beauty depended on the riches and status of its wearer. King Henry, for example, when he needed money, put into pawn at Hereford several great brooches worth 10 marks each, as well as forty smaller ones worth only $4\frac{1}{2}$ marks each.[1] Such brooches were one of the usual presents of the time, and even the stricter moralists agreed that women could accept them without shame if they were given and received openly. In fact such gifts were little more than a polite token of hospitality. When Sir John de la Haye visited the Countess Eleanor at Dover at the beginning of August he had his son with him, and both young Eleanor and Amaury de Montfort presented the boy with brooches. As was fitting Amaury's was much more expensive than his sister's, 44s 8d as compared to a mere 15s.[2]

Both men and women wore tunics with brooches at the neckline, but the woman's tunic was made with tighter sleeves than that of the man. During the thirteenth century her sleeves began to be buttoned from elbow to wrist, explaining the appearance of buttons on the accounts. These buttons might be silver or gilt, and later were often made of coral. However the purchase of nine dozen buttons for the household of young Henry and his sister at Christmas time suggests a generous use of them, perhaps as ornaments.[3]

The tunic was held in place by a girdle, or narrow belt.

Here, too, the rich displayed their wealth with girdles of elegant materials. The silk girdle that the countess of Leicester bought for Amaury was a very modest example. For her marriage to Gilbert de Clare, Joanna, the daughter of Edward I, had a magnificent girdle of gold, adorned with rubies and emeralds, which had been bought in Paris for the enormous sum of £37 12s.[1] The Master of Sherborne Hospital mentioned three girdles in his will, and they were all of silk with gold thread, and ornamented with silver gilt.[2] As the thirteenth century progressed it became fashionable to replace the knotted girdle with a belt which had a metal buckle and pendent tag known as a belt-chape. These were worn by women as well as by men, and gradually became more elaborate. From this belt, or girdle, the lady of the house would hang her keys and purse, or hanging pocket.

The super-tunic, or surcoat, was of the same general nature as the tunic, but was shorter with wide, loose sleeves, and frequently fur-lined. The man's super-tunic was sometimes slit down from the neck and up from the knee to allow greater freedom of movement. However, this garment came in many different styles as a man's surcoat, like a woman's, could be sleeveless and quite long.

The mantle was the necessary outer garment, made from an almost circular piece of material, fastened at the neck by a brooch or a chain. It too was lined with fur to provide insulation against damp and cold. The poor, or stingy, could make one mantle serve for many years. Jacques de Vitry tells the story of the close-fisted knight who upbraided his servant loudly for not finding his mantle quickly enough after a dinner in another knight's hall. The knight asked so sarcastically if he did not know the mantle, that the servant was goaded to reply at the top of his voice: "I have known it well for seven years, Lord, but I cannot find it." In the usual dénouement of medieval stories, the stingy knight became the butt of the assembly, who despised penury, or even common thrift.[3]

The length of a man's clothes depended to a great extent on his social rank. Kings are usually shown in long gowns, nobles in gowns to the ankle, while the merchant's and professional man's tunic only came to mid-calf. Occupation was also a deciding factor. Naturally the workman or labourer in the fields wore a knee-length tunic, if indeed he had not stripped to his breeches. These breeches, which are excellently portrayed in some of the manuscript illuminations, were the special prerogative of the man—hence the derogatory comment, "she wears the breeches in that house". Breeches were made of linen and cut rather like pyjama-trousers, with a large casing at the waist holding a heavy running-string, known as the breech-girdle. The legs were so made that the lower ends could be pulled up to shorten them, and then fastened by a string to the girdle. By the thirteenth century these loose and bulky breeches were only found among the lower classes. Underwear, for men higher in the social scale, had become linen drawers. The woman's underwear, on the other hand, consisted solely of the long chemise, also in linen. The countess of Leicester seems to have had some sort of undergarment of leather, for which the skins were bought by Hicque her tailor, who also purchased three ells of canvas for the same purpose.[1] What use was made of these purchases is something of a puzzle. The Latin word used is *cruralia*, which suggests shin-coverings, and it is possible that the countess's tailor was making her some form of rudimentary riding-breeches or puttees. The countess would often ride astride and need such protection.

Another puzzling garment was the nightgown mentioned in the account of John of Brabant. A nightgown was an unusual item in the thirteenth century and may have been more in the nature of a dressing-gown. Yet when John forgot his at Berwick he attached so much importance to it that a horse was sent specially to bring it to him at Jedburgh.[2] The general practice was to sleep naked, but the manuscript illuminations often picture the sleepers in some form of garment, probably the under chemise.

Hose had become longer and more important. They stretched well above the knee and had a wide top, so that the breeches, or drawers, could be tucked into them, while a cord secured them to the breech-girdle. Apparently there were certain variations in style, for Jordan of Saxony* speaks disdainfully in one of his sermons of a man wearing pleated hose, as if these were the mark of a dandy.[1] Ordinarily the hose were fairly well-shaped and tight below the knee. They were usually made of burnet, but Richard de Montfort had some of russet for his journey to Bigorre.[2] According to the illuminations stockings were of many colours, with green, blue and orange the most common. Women's hose had to be fastened differently from those of the men, because of the absence of breeches. A lady wore a garter just below the knee – not a detail to be seen in most dignified pictures or statues. By the middle of the century some of the hose had developed into a kind of slipper, with a sole of leather fitted to them.

Boots and shoes were of several styles. There was the mid-calf boot, used mainly for rough outdoor work; and a low boot, generally worn by men. There was also a low shoe, common to both sexes, and finally a kind of house shoe, which was cut out over the instep and had a strap which fastened across the ankle. The styles are best understood by comparing the various types in contemporary illustrations. Colour had also come in for shoes at many levels in society. Jacques de Vitry has a pleasant story of the old peasant who always put on his red shoes for every feast day, which he knew by long experience. In this way he reminded his neighbours when they were entitled to a holiday.[3] The poor might hope to receive shoes as alms, if

* Jordan of Saxony was the second master-general of the Dominicans. He preached this sermon while he was in England in 1230 for the first provincial chapter.

they were not among the members of a household which cared for them. Henry III's Liberate Rolls refer to several hundred pairs – at an average cost of 4½d – distributed by the royal almoner before great feasts.[1] This price corresponds to the cost of shoes in the countess's account; hose were more expensive, usually about 10d.

Coverings for the head were worn inside and out, by both men and women. Most men wore the usual linen coif, designed like a more ample skull cap and tied by strings under the chin. These coifs could be quite plain, but the young favoured gay embroidered ones. Since most knights and men of substance wore their hair long and slightly curled at the neck, the coif helped to keep the hair tidy during their active days. Only a young girl appeared bareheaded. She could wear her hair long and loose, with perhaps a chaplet of flowers or a gilt circlet as her only adornment. The older woman wore a veil, and frequently a wimple as well. The wimple was a piece of linen which covered the neck and went under the chin; originally white, later it was also coloured.

Much money and time was spent by the women on these head-dresses, and naturally the moralists found them a fertile field for their complaints about luxury in dress. Berthold of Regensburg, the thirteenth-century German preacher, was quite furious about the unnecessary time and trouble that women put into their garments. Disgustedly, he complained:

All that wherewith you busy yourselves is naught but vanity. You busy yourselves with your veils, you twitch them hither, you twitch them thither; you gild them here and there with gold thread, and spend thereon all your time and trouble. You will spend a good six months' work on a single veil which is sinful great travail – and all that men may praise thy dress.[2]

Berthold would have been appalled at the head-dress Joanna, King Edward's daughter, wore for her marriage, for it was made of gold, wrought with rubies and emeralds (like her

143

girdle), and cost £12 40s.[1] Robert Mannyng was less violent, but more uncomplimentary, about the matter of women's head-dresses. He objected to the saffron wimples and kerchiefs, because they left an unsuspecting man uncertain whether he was looking at a yellowed wimple, or merely a yellowed skin.[2]

Because of the amount of time spent out of doors adequate coverings were needed to protect the elegant coifs and wimples. Hoods, worn by both men and women, and caps were general wear for protection against the weather. The guild of the Cappers, whose articles date from March 1270, defined very carefully the kinds of wool which their members might use. The articles warned against the common fraud of dyeing an old cap black, and reselling it as new. This particular sharp practice was soon detected, as the colour ran in the rain.[3]

Luxurious clothes were one of the pleasures of the rich, and a recognized mark of their status, so the strictures of the moralists were not seriously heeded. The great barons dressed themselves and their children as gorgeously as they could afford. The children of King Edward had caps of peacock feathers, gilded buttons – both for their clothes and the saddles of their horses – and gloves with the arms of the king embroidered on the thumb.[4] Heavy gloves were used by labourers for all kinds of rough work, but elegant gloves were a mark of the rich and were often given as presents. At the end of July the Countess Eleanor bought a dozen pairs for herself and her daughter at the reasonable price of a penny a pair.[5]

Jewelry added to the splendid effect for the rich. Apart from the necessary brooches the most usual article of jewelry was the gold ring, which sometimes had an added stone, usually a diamond, emerald, or sapphire. Rings varied widely in price, and a magnate might own a great number, some of which he used for gifts. Bogo de Clare bought twenty-four gold rings at one time; one dozen cost him 2s each, and the other dozen 2s 4d.[1] These were undoubtedly quite plain and intended for gifts to the relatively unimportant. In young Henry's account the esquire of Anthony Bek, the redoubtable bishop of Durham, was given a ring worth 6s for bringing a palfrey from his master to the king's son; but the wife of the man from whom Henry's household had received stable rights at Guildford got a ring worth only 2s.[2] Obviously gold rings were not merely a common mark of wealth, they also appeared in reasonable numbers in the wills of quite ordinary people. Such rings could hardly be compared with the seventy-eight King Henry put in pawn at Hereford, for the large sum of 200 marks.[3]

Precious stones had a special allegorical significance for medieval man, and different stones had different properties. Bartholomew the Englishman specially favoured the sapphire as the best among the precious stones, "for it was most like heaven in fair weather".[4]

A French song of the thirteenth century describing the wares of a travelling merchant gives some idea of the wide range of small luxuries which added to the elegance of dress. The cheerful pedlar sings the praises of his extraordinarily varied stock: girdles and gloves, pins and needles, linen kerchiefs with flowers or birds embroidered on them, saffron wimples, brooches and buckles – and this was only part of his assortment. Included in his list is a surprisingly up-to-date and comprehensive series of beauty aids for a lady's toilet: "razors, tweezers, looking-glasses, tooth-brushes and tooth-picks, bandeaus and curling-irons, ribbons, combs, mirrors, rose-water . . . cotton with which they rouge, and whitening with which they whiten themselves."[5] Such wares could also be a great deal more elegant than those purchased from an itinerant merchant. In 1297 King Edward's daughter Eleanor gave her father a Christmas present of a portable dressing-box with a comb, a silver-gilt enamelled mirror, and a silver bodkin, all carefully packed in a leather case.[6]

The mirrors perhaps call for some explanation. They

appear to have been reasonably common, at least in France, as in a list of goods traded at Narbonne in the thirteenth century they were included among the domestic items and reckoned by the hundreds.[1] They are rare in the thirteenth-century English accounts, and expensive. In 1292 Henry of Lancaster, King Edward's nephew, bought a new mirror for 2s, after his barber had tried to mend a broken one.[2] These mirrors were small, usually circular, and mounted in a case, made of wood, metal, or the elegant carved ivory of a later century. A charming example, which probably belonged to one of the step-brothers or step-sisters of Henry III, has the arms of England and Lusignan quartered in red and blue on a silver-gilt background.[3] Mirrors were normally made of polished steel, but they were occasionally true looking-glasses, that is, a sheet of glass over a polished metal surface. On one leaf of the Luttrell Psalter, the illustrator has pictured the lady of the house combing her long hair while the serving maid holds the mirror.[4] The little scene is an illustration of the everyday use of the mercer's wares.

Both the merchandise listed and the complaints of the moralists suggest that spending money to be fashionable was as common in the upper classes of the thirteenth century as in most other periods; but the fashions were rather more colourfully expressed, particularly among the men. The competition in elegant clothing in France was so great that St Louis' son passed a special law in 1279 restricting great nobles to not more than five furred robes a year. Others, of lower class, could have even fewer; a bourgeois who had 1,000 *livres* capital might have only one new robe a year, though his wife might have two.[5] But in general even so austere a ruler as St Louis was willing to see his nobles make a reasonable expenditure on clothes so that their wives might love them better, and their men esteem them more. The saintly king quoted the good advice:

He said that men ought to clothe and arm their bodies in such wise that men of worth and age would never say, this man has

146

done too much, nor young men say, this man has done too little.[1]
It all sounds rather like Polonius's advice to Laertes, and it
is this impression of richness, settled order and elegance
which best sums up the whole thirteenth-century attitude
towards clothes.

It is impossible to leave the subject of thirteenth-century
clothes without at least a brief glimpse at armour. Unfortunately it is a highly technical subject and one on which the
experts are much divided about details, but certain general
conclusions are possible. The domestic accounts of the century
are naturally silent on the subject, but it is impossible to visualize a baronial household without the armour and fighting
equipment that formed such an important element in its life.

The basic piece of armour was the hauberk, or tunic, of
chain mail, which usually came to mid-calf. The hauberk
had full-length sleeves, ending in mail mittens. These had a
slit at the wrist, like a woman's long glove, allowing a knight
to slip his hands free without disarming completely. The
hauberk usually had an attached coif of mail, which fitted
under the helmet and could also be easily slipped off when
resting. Besides the protection provided by the hauberk, the
legs were covered by mail stockings and shoes, also made in
one piece, and pulled under the hauberk to fasten to the
breech-girdle.

In the mid-thirteenth century, the helmet was usually the
plain barrel type, with a narrow opening for vision and a
series of air holes below the eye slit. It greatly restricted a
knight's field of vision, and indeed a blow which shifted his
helmet must have rendered him as totally blinded as if he
were playing blindman's buff. This great helmet frequently
had a ring on top so that it could be suspended from a hook
on the saddle when not in immediate use; it also had
carrying-strings. Since helmets were unwieldy and heavy,
they were often carried in the provision carts, along with
the extra hauberks.

Under this chain-mail and heavy helmet, the knight needed further protection to take the weight of the blows and prevent the chain mail from embedding itself in the flesh. There was a special guild of linen armourers who specialized in making the necessary under-garments, complete over-garments (such as were sometimes used in tournaments), and also padded linings for helmets.

The special mark of the knight was the great belt which supported his heavy sword and its scabbard. In fact, when describing the making of a knight, the term always used in England in the thirteenth century was "conferring the belt of knighthood". Besides his armour, a sword, a lance, and a shield, the knight needed a horse strong enough to carry this heavy load and trained to behave properly in battle. The destrier, or warhorse, was encouraged to greater speed by the long prick-spurs strapped over the knight's mail stockings. To equip oneself as a knight was exceedingly expensive, and the price of equipment was a heavy burden for the lesser baron whose cash income never seemed to keep pace with his expenses.

Armour, like clothes, often formed part of legacies. When Bartholomew de Legh died around 1230, he left his shield and helmet and banner to the cemetery of St Edmund, but a hauberk and mailed shoes to the earl of Winchester. Another small hauberk, with a mail coif, went to W. Bordel, while his nephew got a hauberk, mail stockings, and a mail covering – perhaps for the horse – all of which Bartholomew himself had earlier inherited from his brother.[1] Although capable of lasting for long periods, chain mail was particularly liable to rust, and was very difficult to keep in good condition, so a prudent knight took particular care of his valuable investment. In the account for the works at the earl of Cornwall's castle of Wallingford, two men were paid 6s for polishing the arms twice a year; seven bushels of bran were bought for polishing, and also for storing the arms.[2] Another method employed for cleaning chain mail was to

148

put it in a barrel or leather bag with sand and vinegar, then the container was rolled and shaken to remove the rust. Such cleaning was absolutely necessary to prevent the armour's rapid decay.

Only the fortunate knight had complete armour; the ordinary fighting-man was less well protected. Some had hauberks of chain mail, but others had only linen armour or *cuir bouilli*, made of thick leather which had been boiled in oil or water. While the leather was soft it was moulded to the required shape and then allowed to cool and dry, when it became extremely hard. Frequently the fighting man had a battle hat, often of iron, which was round with a flat brim and like the knight's helmet, had carrying-strings for convenience.

Medieval weapons and machines are well described in many books on medieval warfare, but it is important to remember that such items were of real interest to all the household of a great baron. An important magnate often made every effort to incorporate all the most modern improvements into the defences of his castles. This interest in defence is particularly marked in the accounts of the countess of Leicester and of Roger Leyburn during the Barons' War. Both these accounts emphasize the important place of the thirteenth-century engineer who was the consulting expert of his time. The countess mentions Master William, who had been specifically engaged to improve the fortifications of the castles under the earl of Leicester's control, particularly Kenilworth. He was obviously a highly-regarded technician, and was well paid when he was dismissed at the end of August.[1] Roger Leyburn included generous sums to Master Peter the engineer and his assistants when he detailed the expenses for his campaign in Sandwich. Master Peter was responsible for strengthening the brattice, or wooden parapet, and supervising the preparation of stones for the catapult, while Imbert de Montferrant was paid £6 12s 4d for repairing a special siege engine.[2] Technical skill seems to have been generously rewarded.

9

Travel and Transport

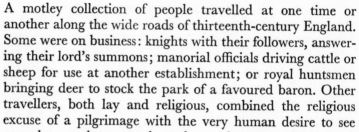

A motley collection of people travelled at one time or another along the wide roads of thirteenth-century England. Some were on business: knights with their followers, answering their lord's summons; manorial officials driving cattle or sheep for use at another establishment; or royal huntsmen bringing deer to stock the park of a favoured baron. Other travellers, both lay and religious, combined the religious excuse of a pilgrimage with the very human desire to see new places and new people, and were the unsung forerunners of Chaucer's unforgettable band. The roads were also worn by the passage of goods. There were the packhorses, driven by grooms and laden with almost any variety of merchandise; the slow-moving carts whose freight might be as unwieldy as a tun of wine. This traffic was occasionally increased by the retinue of a great baron moving his household from one manor or castle to another, or by the enormous, straggling royal train which frequently perambulated the realm.

The immobility of medieval people has been exaggerated. Evidence continues to accumulate showing a much greater shift and mobility among larger sections of the population than had previously been believed. It has always been recognized that the king's court was often on the move, creating a tremendous problem for the royal provisioners and the others in charge; but the household of a great magnate, such as the earl of Leicester or the bishop of Hereford, was almost as peripatetic as that of the king. In this matter, as in so many others, the barons copied as far as was appropriate the manners and methods of the king.

In fact no picture of a thirteenth-century baronial household would be complete or accurate without an account of its problems of travel and transport. Travel was frequent and there was a constant need to transport household goods from one place to another, and to deliver purchases made at the great fairs or from the London merchants. The marshal was the household official charged with the major responsibility for this department of domestic life, and he was fully occupied. One of the marshal's duties was to arrange with the reeve of the nearest demesne manor about the supplies needed for the horses. The reeve received a tally from the marshal for the bran and oats, hay and forage delivered from the manor to the stable of the household. These supplies were later credited to the reeve's account when the auditors came round to check the yearly account of the issues of the manor. In the same way the marshal also gave the reeve a tally for the horseshoes and nails he received from him, and then the marshal provided the steward with the particulars of their use. In fact without the steward's permission the marshal was not allowed to use such local supplies to shoe any stranger's horse.[1]

The countess of Leicester's account follows the normal pattern of the household account of its time and considers the items answered for by the marshal as an integral part of every day's reckoning. They followed immediately on the items listed for the kitchen, and also included the number of horses in the stable. Part of the marshal's duty was to inform the steward every night of this number, so that it could duly be inserted in the account.

In the royal household, and probably in any baronial household as large as that of the Leicesters, more than one official was needed to deal with the stables. Besides the marshal, there might also be a clerk of the marshalcy who bought hay, oats, straw, and horseshoes when such purchases were necessary. He was furnished with the money to pay these suppliers, and also paid the wages of the grooms and those in charge of the sumpters. Another minor official looked after the sumpters and the carts. He was responsible for estimating the continuing usefulness of the horses; when the treasurer and the steward had agreed that they were worn out, this official saw that they were given to the almoner, and new ones purchased. Besides checking on the condition of the horses, this official had to buy the carts, sacks, trunks, and other equipment for the sumpters.[1]

The countess's account illustrates the perennial fact that practice is never as tidy as theory. Several of the named servants seem to have a connection with the provisions for, and the expenses of, the horses and the carts, but their functions are seldom clearly defined. Colin the Marshal's name does explain his office, although he does not carry on his duties during the early part of the account, because he had been sent off to Amaury de Montfort.[2] Once at Dover, however, Colin was busy with the many expenses for the horses. Since there were fewer manorial supplies on which to draw, his duties were more difficult. In July, he had to travel as far as Canterbury looking for iron for horseshoes or for the carts.[3] Apart from Colin, Walter the Clerk frequently bought the oats, and Richard Gobion was charged with the payment of many items for the horse and the carts.[4]

Another Colin, Colin the Smith, was added to the countess's household at Easter, and was paid 2s on his wages in July. The clerk of the roll noted that Colin had entered the countess's service without an agreement.[5] The smith was a most necessary member of the household and was kept busy caring for the shoeing of the horses and the fitting of iron to the carts. When possible, he kept and re-worked the old horseshoes, which had been cast, as this made the new shoes not only cheaper but also tougher. Of course there were fraudulent smiths and, according to the preachers, some of them were particularly ingenious. Jacques de Vitry tells the story of the smith who used to put a nail or a needle in the foot of a pilgrim's or a traveller's horse when he shod them.

152

After the stranger had gone a mile or two and his horse had become thoroughly lame, an agent of the smith would appear by the road and offer to buy the horse for a tiny sum, just enough to cover the value of the hide and the shoes. The traveller, afraid of losing contact with his companions, would accept the offer; the horse would then be returned to the smith who took out the needle, rested the horse, and sold it for an enormous profit.[1] A household avoided such unfortunate incidents by having their own smith who could be trusted.

Although the legal treatises and the account give some idea of the administrative factors which allowed a large household to be so mobile, they give little idea of the nature of travel. The medieval road has been excessively maligned. Undoubtedly, there was little planned building of new roads during the Middle Ages, but the old Roman roads were in better condition than during the eighteenth century. For one thing there was not so much wheeled traffic; for another the roads were so wide that different kinds of travellers could normally pass without exasperation or delay. The standard set for road width required that sixteen armed knights should be able to ride side by side, two wagons could pass, or two oxherds could just make their long goads touch.[2]

This question of the width of the road was often disputed. In a case at Winchcombe in 1245 the rector wanted to lengthen and enlarge his church, but the abbot objected. He feared that it would narrow the road too much for the abbey carts, especially those carrying timber. The jury was also afraid that too great an extension would prevent two carts passing; and this would be harmful to the town, especially at fair-time, it added firmly. The king's final decision tried to satisfy everyone. He allowed the rector to extend the church, but the road to the abbey was to remain thirty feet broad, and the highway itself eighteen feet.[3] Since the case disappears, probably all the plaintiffs accepted this as a reasonable compromise. Underbrush from wooded lands encroaching on the highway also cut down on the road's width, and was a possible source of lurking danger. At Kenilworth, the king gave orders to have the forest cut back, as it encroached on the main highway between Coventry and Warwick, and provided too easy cover for those rogues who would break the king's peace.[1]

The existence of a network of roads in thirteenth-century England is shown by the maps of Matthew Paris, the great chronicler. He was a man of many interests and talents, and his maps of England and Scotland are more than mere diagrams. They are a genuine attempt at a real map, oriented to the north, and showing some idea of the importance of scale. Matthew based them on an itinerary from Dover to Berwick by way of Newcastle, but drew this on a north-south line, so that Dover, Canterbury, and Rochester were due south of London. Students of medieval cartography insist, however, that at this time distortion for a specific purpose was considered quite legitimate, so the placing of Dover at the centre bottom of the map was not so much due to ignorance as to the desire to emphasize the northern route.[2] Matthew's *Scema Britanniae*, in his *Liber Additamentorum*, also illustrates, though inaccurately, the four main Roman roads of Britain.

By the time of the Gough Map, in the middle of the fourteenth century, a far more sophisticated representation was possible. In Matthew Paris's work the itinerary was really more important than the topography. The Gough Map, on the other hand, was relatively accurate and realistic; designed for the use of travellers, it may have been kept at a central location where it could be easily consulted. It traces five main roads radiating from London; to Exeter, Bristol, St David's, Carlisle, and to Doncaster and beyond by the old north road. It also testifies to a major road from Bristol to Chester, and another from Southampton along the Channel coast, through Chichester, Lewes, Winchelsea, Rye, and up to Canterbury.[3] The itineraries of the thirteenth-century kings show that, besides these well-recognized main routes, there was everywhere in central England a network of secondary roads which were quite adequate for even the heavy loads of the king's retinue.

The real problem in medieval travel was the scarcity of bridges. Indeed the importance of bridges and fords for medieval travel is underlined by some of the places named on Matthew Paris's maps, which owe their inclusion solely to their usefulness as crossing places of rivers; a knowledge of their location was essential to travellers. The repair and upkeep of bridges was expensive but most necessary. Usually this was a local responsibility, but the king could step in to enforce payment when all other measures failed. Thus the men of the county of Chester were required to repay the royal exchequer £20 19s 2½d for the repair of the bridge at Chester. This amount had been paid by a royal justice, even though the men of the county had been liable for such repairs from the time of the Domesday Book.[1] Leaving money in one's will for the building or upkeep of a local bridge was considered a laudable charitable bequest, though charity was not always as powerful a motive as it might have been. For example the will of Martin of Holy Cross, Master of Sherborne Hospital, proved him a man of great possessions, but he left only half a mark for the repair of the bridge at Totton.[2]

Bridges might also be destroyed for strategic reasons, as was shown by the Lord Edward's activities in the weeks before Evesham. The king's son was trying to keep Simon de Montfort and his army isolated west of the Severn, and therefore ordered all the bridges over the Severn to be destroyed, including the main one at Worcester. The little boats, normally to be found along the water's edge, were pulled away and even the fords were spoiled by having ditches dug across them. These were the harsh measures of war, but they underline the relative ease with which the transport system could be disrupted. Even in peacetime the scarcity of bridges or passable fords often brought destruction or death, especially in times of high water. Thus Simon de Montfort had his carts, horses, and one of his men washed away near Dorking in 1250. All the goods in the carts disappeared; nevertheless, the king optimistically ordered the sheriff of Surrey to find the goods and deliver them to the earl's bailiff.[1]

Despite any difficulties on the road or the breakdown of bridges, the people of the thirteenth century travelled extensively, though at varying speeds. The large household obviously journeyed far more slowly than the merchant or the messenger. A great household was usually accompanied by an extensive retinue, as well as by a number of carts and sumpter-horses, and the problems of accommodation and supplies were intensified. The household could carry some of the necessary provisions, but it was also burdened with furniture and the valuables of the wardrobe. If the journey were long, special arrangements had to be made for a place to sleep, as most inns were not big enough to harbour such a large company. The usual practice was to dispatch servants charged with arranging shelter at a castle or monastery convenient to the route. This need to keep to a predetermined itinerary, as well as the slowness of the accompanying carts, tended to delay baronial travellers.

Some estimate of the average distance covered in a day by such a household can be gained from the countess of Leicester's account in February; when the household was at Wallingford, it moved on to Odiham by way of Reading, spending one night there.[2] The journey on each of these days was just over fifteen miles, the normal pace of such a move in midwinter. But in June, when the countess had to hurry across country with her household to the greater safety of Dover castle, she consistently travelled thirty miles a day.[3] This may reasonably be considered as fast as such a large company could move, and the sustained rate of speed hints at the urgency that drove them on.

All thirteenth-century travellers did not of course belong to large retinues, and small groups with good horses travelled much faster. The merchant could do between thirty-five and forty miles a day, travelling only in the daylight hours, if his merchandise was light and easily carried on one horse. Freight services, such as commonly transported wine in England or travelled the Alpine passes with goods from Italy for the fairs of Champagne, were among the slowest of all traffic. Fastest of all was the messenger, for he also travelled at night and often requisitioned extra horses along his route. He might cover as much as fifty-five to sixty miles a day.[1]

The countess's account is particularly full of references to messengers, and accentuates their important place in her household at this particular time. Messengers were thrown into unusual prominence by the constant need for communication between the earl in the west of England and the countess at Odiham or Dover. They carried back and forth the news of the changing fortunes of the two main bodies of baronial supporters, and Gobithesti, Slingawai and Trubodi are constantly named in the account. Unfortunately it is not possible to determine their distances and times exactly, but the roll shows Gobithesti, for example, making three trips from Odiham to the west of England in the month of May alone. He went once to Cardiff; once to find the earl when his exact location was unknown to the account clerk, although Simon was in fact at Hereford; and finally to Hereford again.[2] The length and frequency of these trips make it obvious that messengers could continuously cover long distances in a reasonably short time.

In the royal household the permanent messengers formed a recognized group of servants. They were provided with horses, given their yearly robes and shoes, and were ranked above the casual grooms, but below the squires and serjeants.[3] It is reasonable to suggest that the messengers of a baronial household, lay or ecclesiastic, occupied the same relative place in their smaller hierarchy. Thus in the bishop of

Hereford's account the winter wages of John his messenger are duly included at the rate of 2s 6d, the amount paid the lesser serjeants, and 6d more than that received by the grooms.[1] Besides wages, messengers received their expenses. The bishop of course was liable to heavy expenditure for his messenger who had to go to Rome on episcopal business, since the expenses for one trip came to 50s;[2] but the countess of Leicester's expenses for her messengers in England alone were also heavy – over 35s for the seven month period of the roll. In quieter times, Bogo de Clare paid only 3s 6d for the expenses of his messengers from Christmas to Easter.[3]

These travelling expenses were reckoned according to rank. A knight was entitled to 2s 6d a day, when he was absent from the household, while a clerk or squire would receive 1s 6d if he had two horses, and only 1s if he travelled with one horse. Lesser officials with only one horse had to be content with 4½d a day.[4] This appears to have been a generally accepted scale, and tallies with the amounts paid to the countess's servants and officials for their expenses.

The essential for all this travel was the horse, which varied in type and value in strict relation to the social status of its rider. At the top of the scale was the great warhorse of the knight which might cost the almost astronomical sum of £40 to £80.[5] This was one of the heaviest investments that a knight was forced to make, and helps to explain the enthusiasm for tournaments, since the horses and armour of the defeated knights became the property of their conquerors – a truly rich and useful prize. Naturally the warhorse was not wasted on everyday service. Usually the knight rode a palfrey, while his squire or serving-man led the great warhorse in readiness for military use. These beasts were specially prized for their ability to carry the enormous load of a man in full armour, so that massive strength was the primary consideration. The Shire and the Belgian draught horses of the present day are the lineal descendants of the great medieval warhorse.

The ordinary rouncey, which was used by the average fighting-man, cost a great deal less than a warhorse; it ranged in price from 40s to 5 marks, i.e. 66s 8d,[1] and even that was a major expense for the often impecunious man-at-arms. The palfrey was the everyday saddle horse of the upper classes. It also varied greatly in price, depending on its quality, but was generally more expensive than the rouncey. The range of price witnessed by the Liberate Rolls, for example, extends from 5 marks to £27 for a specially valuable animal bought as a royal gift for one of the favourite Poitevins.[2] The average price seems to have been about 10 marks.[3] But accurate statistics are impossible from the fragmentary reports that have come down to us, and as always with medieval prices it is dangerous to draw firm conclusions. Thus the clerk of Bogo de Clare's account lists two horses bought at exactly the same price – one was a palfrey for the lord and the other merely a cart-horse, yet both cost 106s 8d.[4] All the same there was as a general rule a considerable difference in the prices of the horses which roughly correspond to the use to which they were put.

Because horses played such a vital part in a baron's own life, as well as providing necessary services for the household, much thought and discussion revolved around the ways to choose a good horse, and the best methods of curing his diseases. The thirteenth century produced an excellent manual on horses by Albert the Great, the brilliant German Dominican and teacher of Thomas Aquinas. His treatise on horses was part of a general scientific work on natural history, for Albert was much more interested in science than his better-known pupil. When he discussed horses he drew on practical experience as well as scientific theories; as he came from a noble family this interest and knowledge would have been a natural part of his early education. He tried to provide a summary of the ways to judge a horse, as well as describing the approved methods of treating its illnesses.[5] His standards for the various points of the outstanding horse was accepted for several centuries; in fact Shakespeare's description of Adonis' excellent horse carefully mentions the points emphasized by Albert the Great three centuries before.

The thirteenth-century baron was interested not only in the quality and care of his horse, but also in the elegance of its trappings. In normal times the horse eloquently displayed its owner's wealth and position. The warhorse's trappings served a practical purpose, for it was often protected by linen-armour, or even by chain-mail, which covered head and neck, forequarters and hindquarters, and extended all the way to the hocks; this to some extent protected the horse in battle, and also ensured that no adversary could seize the bridle and thus capture the rider. Nevertheless their weight and length would be likely to make him stumble on a crowded battlefield. Thirteenth-century trappings do not seem to have been decorated with armorial bearings, as became common later, but the illuminators picture them most colourfully – green lined with red, for example.[1]

In times of peace, and for social occasions, elegance took precedence over protection. The queen was given 23s 5d for jewelled saddle-bows, orphreys – or borders – and fringe for her saddle on Whitsun, 1237.[2] John of Brabant mentioned in his account his expenses for gilded spurs, and for a saddle with the insignia of his father, Godfrey of Brabant.[3] Saddles were often adorned in this way, and gilded as well. Bogo de Clare had a gilded saddle for himself with the arms of Gaston de Bearn on it, and twelve saddles for his companions were also worked with the same arms.[4] This practice of having the arms of another lord on your saddle seems to have been a special mark of courtesy towards a man whom you wished to honour. In any case Bogo de Clare spared no expense in keeping his horse, and those of his retinue, elegantly arrayed. There are frequent mentions of gilded saddles, embroidery for the saddles, and silver ornaments.[5] Even the children of the great shared to some extent in this display. A dozen gilded buttons were bought to decorate the saddles of young

Henry, Edward I's son, and his cousin, John of Brittany.[1] No such glamorous items appear on the more utilitarian accounts of the bishop of Hereford and the countess of Leicester. Their horse-cloths are made of rough and practical materials, designed for protection rather than elegance.

Although the centre of the stage was taken by the great warhorses with their long trappings, and the elegant palfreys with their gilded and decorated saddles, the key role in the economy was played by the unromantic and hardworking sumpter-horses and cart-horses who provided the transport for goods. Sumpter-horses could carry a surprising amount. For example it took only one horse to take the expensive supply of spices and dates from Odiham to Kenilworth for the use of Richard of Cornwall,[2] while the heavy purchases of cloth in London in May were brought back to Odiham on four horses.[3] The description of Becket's impressive procession through the towns of France gives an unusual prominence to the accompanying sumpter-horses,[4] but they were always the inevitable concomitant to medieval travelling.

To facilitate packing and handling, certain sumpter-horses were often assigned to specific duties. In the household of Bogo de Clare, one sumpter-horse carried the bed, one the wardrobe and one the buttery.[5] This was an inescapable minimum, for the sumpters which carried the equipment of Joanna, King Edward's daughter, on her marriage to the earl of Gloucester numbered seven. They included one for the kitchen furniture, one for the candles, and one for all the requirements of the chapel.[6]

The heaviest and bulkiest loads were carried by the carts. The countess of Leicester had a long cart and a small long cart, according to her clerk's somewhat ambiguous description. In May she bought a new cart bound with iron, at a cost of less than 33s, since that figure also included some repairs.[7] Through all the household accounts reference is made to the expenses for these carts: new saddles for the cart horses, new reins, grease for the creaking axles, and various reinforcing irons. When the baron's own supply of carts was insufficient to provide for the transport of wine, cloths, or the harness of the household, others were rented.

Carts were made of local timber, and the most expensive thing about them was their wheels and their iron fittings. The wheel was made of a rim of timber, firmly morticed together and with spokes radiating from the hub to the rim. The wheels were bound with separate pieces of iron called strakes, which were fastened to the wood with great nails known as strake-nails. These strake-nails had projecting heads, and when they were worn down could be replaced. The Luttrell Psalter shows a typical two-wheeled farm-cart, with the heavy iron binding on the wheels, being forced up an improbably right-angled hill.[1] The irons must have made movement of the carts much easier on muddy or slippery ground, but it was the weight of these heavy iron wheels with their projecting nails that helped to destroy the medieval road. Carts also had clouts – thin, flat pieces of iron which seem to have been used to strengthen the axle-hole, and perhaps were also nailed on as an extra reinforcement at points of extreme wear. These were of much lighter iron than the heavy binding for the wheels.[2]

Carting service was easily maintained, and fairly cheap, even in troubled times. The countess paid 33s for the carriage of six tuns of wine from Southampton to Odiham, a cost of about 1½d a mile per tun[3] – not excessive for the most awkward of all loads. At the end of May two carts were rented at London to take two tuns of wine to Kenilworth, at a cost of only 18s 6d for the ninety-five mile trip. It was obviously a normal part of the economy to rent carts as well as horses, and frequent references to this practice are to be found in all the accounts of the time. When the countess of Leicester was faced with the task of moving the belongings of her household on to Dover, her baggage train was headed by Hicque the Tailor who was in charge of twelve men and four carts each drawn by three horses. In addition she rented two more carts in Porchester.[1] Up to about 1285, a carter with his cart could be hired for 4d a day, while a carter alone cost 1d or 2d.[2] None of the frequent references to renting, and its relatively low cost, explain whether this cost included the return of the horse to its starting-place.

The evidence shows that the baronial household of the time would have between thirty and forty horses in its stable. The countess's average was nearer thirty, but hers was a truncated household. However, in times of disturbance, more horses might be needed and would be borrowed or rented. A lady when travelling might use a chariot, a long covered wagon, more elegant than comfortable. The countess of Leicester borrowed the countess of Arundel's chariot to make her trip from Porchester to Dover, and rewarded the driver with 5s for himself and another 5s for his expenses back to Arundel. His expenses were high because the chariot was large enough to require five horses.[3]

The marshal, as the responsible official, had to be prepared to feed the continually fluctuating number of horses which might be stabled at the household's expense. Sometimes the strain was too great, as when in the Leicester household the number of horses in the stable jumped from forty-four on a Sunday to one hundred and seventy-two on Tuesday, and three hundred and thirty-four on Thursday. Admittedly this was due to the arrival of the earl with a large part of his retinue but it is not surprising that the marshal was short of oats on Thursday, and had to go out and buy more than nine quarters for the last arrivals.[4] The system of supply from the nearest manor was tried to breaking-point by such enormous fluctuations.

In addition to horse-drawn traffic, there was transport by sea. Not only did all imported commodities come to England by ship, but within the country shipping was often used for long distance trade to avoid the many dangers, delays and tolls faced in overland transport. At this time English sailors and English merchants did not have the pre-eminence they later gained, and it was primarily foreign shipping that filled English harbours. However whenever possible small boats were used for local trade; especially for bulky or heavy goods. Along the coast, and particularly in such areas as the Cinque Ports, the English shipping trade was important and useful. Boats could also be rented, as carts and horses were, and there are frequent references in the countess's account to this practice.

As the summer of 1265 wore on and the problem of supplying the household in Dover castle became more acute, the means of transport were constantly re-arranged, illustrating the many difficulties. Carts were sent out to seek hay and grass for the horses in the surrounding countryside, as well as the necessary foodstuffs for the household. Boats were also hired to fill the household's needs. Sometimes the boat would bring a load of firewood, a scarce commodity in Dover; or again, it would be sent up the coast to Pevensey to seek a machine needed to strengthen the defences of Dover castle.[1] By August 1st, when that item was paid, the imminence of battle overhung the kingdom.

A delightful picture from a bestiary of a ship beached on a whale's back illustrates the kind of small boat that was in use at this time for coastal shipping. It had an oblong sail and single mast, and was steered not with a rudder but with a steering-oar.[2] Many of the barons of the Cinque Ports were merchants and shipowners at the same time. Salomon Wibert, a merchant of Sandwich from whom the countess of Leicester bought wine and salt, had two ships called *La Reyne* and *La Nicholas*. These ships were worth about £10 with all their tackle, proving that a shipowner could be a man of substance.[3]

The general picture built up from these details about horses and carts, chariots and boats, is one of a civilization adequately equipped for travel and transport. The travel was not necessarily comfortable, but thirteenth-century society was prepared to take certain discomforts for granted. A preacher draws attention to one of the inconveniences of being constantly on the move in his story of the owners of a manor apologizing to their visitors for the lack of some belongings: "Such and such we have not here, because we have sent them before to the place to which we are about to go."[1] The countess's cross-country trips, though made for unusual reasons, were not untypical. All the other household accounts illustrate the accepted social pattern of frequent moves; and, indeed, every member of a great household took this journeying for granted as a natural part of his life.

10

The Amusements of a Baronial Household

No account of the life of a baronial household in the thirteenth century would be complete without at least a passing glimpse at its amusements. The class distinctions, which are so noticeable in other matters, applied here also. Certain sports were reserved to the barons, as privileges of their higher status, and the common pastimes of the peasant and the townsman were considered demeaning and unsuitable. The magnates were particularly interested in two outdoor sports: hunting and the tournament. Indoors, when night or bad weather kept them in their halls, they turned to chess, which was pre-eminently their game, or to tables and dice. At feasts and around the fire they listened to the songs, stories and entertainments of the various types of minstrels. Several wealthy households of the time ensured that music was available when required by having a resident harper. The ladies of the household also went hunting and played games, but embroidery was considered the proper pastime for their leisure, and the accounts tell of the purchase of silk thread for this purpose. Then there were, as there have always been, toys for the children and domestic animals.

Hunting was not only the prime sport of the baronial class, it was also their consuming passion. In fact it was exceedingly popular at all levels of the social scale, but rank defined the kind of game and the places where it was permissible to hunt. The cat, the coney and the hare were hunted by everyone, but the favourite game, restricted to the king and fortunate lords, was the deer. In the thirteenth century the royal forests still covered a great part of England,[1] and preserved the beasts of the forest – the red deer, the fallow deer, the roe deer, and the wild boar – for the king's pleasure. His exclusive rights in these forests were enforced by a whole system of forest law and a hierarchy of forest administrators in addition to the usual provisions of the law. Henry III's ancestors had been compulsive hunters, but it was not such an overriding passion with Henry himself, although he enjoyed staying at the royal lodges of Clarendon and Geddington where the hunting was particularly good.

The barons tried to obtain from the king the coveted grants of "vert and venison" within their lands. When granted this privilege, they had the right to hunt the beasts of the forest and to cut the undergrowth and timber, to administer their own regulations and levy their own fines for poaching. The earl of Leicester had owned one of the best-known of the private forests, that of Leicester, when he acceded to the earldom; but he sold most of it in 1240 to the burgesses of the town for £1,000, since he needed ready money to take on crusade.[1] Odiham, where the earl and countess also had rights of "vert and venison", should have provided them with good hunting, for this was one of the reasons for building a castle there. In happier days the king had often sent them deer with which to stock their parks. A park, or district of land enclosed by a paling, was frequently built by a baron who did not have a private forest, or chase, and who wished to indulge his passion for deer. Such parks needed no royal licence if they did not infringe on the royal forests. They were often ingeniously equipped with 'deer leaps", which encouraged the entrance of deer into the park but made it almost impossible for them to escape. Once the deer had left the royal forest and entered a park or a chase, they were free from the forest law, and could properly be taken. The same principle also applied in reverse. On an autumn day in 1251 Richard, earl of Gloucester, and some of his companions had gone for a walk after dinner in the earl's chase of Micklewood. Earl Richard loosed two of his dogs, who found a hart, pursued it beyond his boundaries, and finally took it within the king's forest. Richard, as an earl, was answerable only to the king, but all his companions were ordered before the justices of the forest for this breach of the law.[1]

Another special privilege of an earl or a baron, recognized by the Charter of the Forest, was the right to take one or two deer for his own use when travelling through a royal forest, although he was only supposed to exercise this right in view of a royal forester or when he had signalled his presence by blowing his horn.[2] However this was a very moderate concession in view of the general passion for game. When the great barons went hunting they often took large numbers of beasts; thus in nine days of July 1252 Richard of Cornwall took thirty-two bucks in the forest of Rockingham.[3] This seems to have been an accepted average, but could easily be exceeded. The unsettled state of the realm in 1264 is reflected in the extreme depredations of that unstable character the young earl of Derby. With a great company of knights and men of position, he invaded the royal forest of the Peak during the summer, taking forty or fifty deer at a time and driving away as many more.[4]

But sport was not the only advantage, for the resulting fresh meat was a welcome luxury. There were two regular seasons for the deer: from June 24th to September 14th, and from November 11th to February 2nd. The summer season was considered superior, as it was the time when the male deer could be taken when they were fat. The meat of the does, taken in the winter, was much leaner. Extra supplies of venison were salted, and kept in store for the rest of the year. Even the poor and the sick might enjoy an occasional taste of venison, for it seems to have been the common practice to give the meat from deer found dead within the royal forest to the needy, the ill, and even to the lepers.[5]

Hunting had its own technical terminology which the children of the well-born were set to learn as part of their basic education. The male and female of both the red deer and the fallow deer were distinguished by special names for each year of each sex. The dogs, too, were carefully categorized. In the early part of the fourteenth century, the current knowledge and practice were put into a brief treatise, called *L'Art de Venerie*, by William Twici, the huntsman of Edward II. His work owes much to his practical experience, and a great deal of its material was copied by later writers.[1]

Huntsmen were often regular members of great baronial households, though they were not so well paid as Twici, who received the extraordinary sum of $7\frac{1}{2}$d a day. Bishop Swinfield's huntsman kept his master's household well supplied with venison, and received 2s 6d in wages, both winter and summer,[2] but the countess of Leicester's account mentions no such permanent servant. Eleanor did pay the daily wages of the huntsmen of her son Guy, during the time she was at Odiham, and the master received 2d a day, and his assistants $1\frac{1}{2}$d. She also paid a lad charged with the special care of her two greyhounds $1\frac{1}{2}$d a day.[3]

Despite the fact that even clerical households employed huntsmen, preachers did not think very highly of the sport. They grudgingly admitted that it was suitable for earls, barons, and knights, but only to keep them from idleness which might lead them to worse sins.[4] Sad stories were told of the hunters who were so enamoured of their sport that they could not break off for meals or mass, and were sucked down to hell in their endless pursuit of the stag.[5] Sometimes the cautionary tales have an unusual twist. Jacques de Vitry tells a delightful anecdote of the monks who were forbidden to eat any meat, except that acquired by hunting. Their passion for meat led them to the ingenious expedient of using dogs to pursue the pigs they were raising in a mock chase through the convent. Thus with casuistical accuracy, they could claim the right to eat the pork.[6]

Though hunting with hounds was the most usual form of the sport, hawking – or hunting with falcons – was one of

169

the chief enthusiasms of the medieval upper-class; the art of falconry was seriously studied. The scientific treatise of the Emperor Frederick II on *The Art of Falconry* is still an important work. The emperor had a wide knowledge of his subject, and a cold, most un-medieval insistence on what he had learned himself through observation and practice. Frederic totally refused to bow to pseudo-authorities whose knowledge was more literary than real. His book is more than a manual of practical instruction; its system and scientific nature make it a valuable contribution to medieval zoology.[1]

The important place which falcons took in the emperor's administrative records, and his passion for the sport of hawking, put the case of the medieval enthusiast at its strongest. They help to make intelligible the action of that bishop of Lincoln who solemnly excommunicated all the inhabitants of a rural deanery who might know where Sir Gerald Salvayn's wandering falcon was, but had not returned it.[2] Such a penalty for a theft, even of a falcon, seems rather out of proportion, but the accounts also illustrate the lengths to which the owner of a prize falcon might go. John of Brabant lost his falcon while riding around Cambridge, and sent Stephen, his falconer, to search for it. The hawk was finally retrieved, but it proved an expensive bird, as it cost John over 36s in expenses. The bird had to be bought back from a man who had bought it from another who had found it – a long, complicated, and costly procedure,[3] yet it was probably worth while, as trained birds were a heavy investment. King Henry's purchases of falcons, in the middle of the century, show that he paid 11 marks for two gerfalcons, while one goshawk cost 100s, and another 15 marks.[4]

The vocabulary of falconry was a precise and specialized one, well known to the medieval upper classes but needing some explanation in the present. The term "falcon" could be used to describe the whole class of birds of prey with short, hooked beaks, strong claws and great destructive power, and also including hawks. The falconer, however, was a great deal more precise. He restricted the use of the term "falcon" to the trained female peregrine, the noblest of all the hunting birds. The male peregrine, smaller and less aggressive, was called the tiercel. As well as an exact terminology, the falconer also observed a strict hierarchy of birds based on the rank of their owner. According to the *Book of St Albans*, a fourteenth-century treatise on falconry, the falcon, i.e. the peregrine, was reserved for the prince and the noble. The yeoman might have a goshawk, while the sporting priest was only allowed a sparrow-hawk, which was still another notch down the scale of birds.[1]

The training of a falcon required constant attention, so that it was usual for its owner to keep his bird with him, on his hand, or to have it occupy a perch in the chamber. During the season of the moult they had to be specially well guarded. King Henry paid as much as 10 marks to have the royal gerfalcons trained, and also provided cranes for them to practise on.[2] John of Brabant, who was less wealthy, could only afford cocks for his falcons.[3] Not only the administrative orders and accounts, but also a surprisingly large literature, mirror the passionate concern of the medieval nobles for the proper care of their birds. A serious scholar, such as the twelfth-century Adelard of Bath, set up a very strict series of requirements for those who had to take care of the diseases of falcons. He insisted that they "not only must be sober, patient, and chaste, alert and of sweet breath, but must avoid those from whom hawks might become infested with vermin".[4] Albert the Great also dealt with falcons in his treatise on animals, but he added little to contemporary knowledge. Much of his information was drawn from Frederick II's treatise, and Albert, like Adelard, was more interested in the birds' diseases than anything else.

The extent of this literature, so surprisingly pragmatic and free from the exaggerated symbolism frequently found in medieval literature, shows the practical nature of the people to whom it was addressed. Falconry passionately interested the king and the magnates, lay and clerical, who loved their sport and constantly looked for new ways to improve it; they also thought highly of their trained servants. Bishop Swinfield's account shows the prominent place in the household accorded to the fowler, Adam Harpin. His wages were 3s 4d, winter and summer, and he had been a trusted servant of the bishops of Hereford for some fifteen years. The previous bishop, Thomas Cantilupe, had given him a dwelling at Ross, subject only to an annual rent of 22d.[1] Harpin had several tasks; in the autumn he was sent out with his nets to catch partridges and other birds, and in June he watched the falcons' eyrie so as to capture the young birds as soon as they were sufficiently fledged to leave the nest.[2]

It is eminently suitable that the proper illustration for the month of May, as characterized by Bartholomew the Englishman in his calendar of symbols for the months of the year, was a young knight riding out for the chase, with his hawk on his wrist.[3] Spring was the merry season for the Middle Ages, and if there was no convenient war then chase or tournament must serve as substitutes.

Although all classes tried to encroach on the baronial sport of hunting, the tournament remained distinctively the amusement of the upper class. Imported from France during the twelfth century, and with many of its rules and customs set by French patterns, the tournament had become established in England though it was not yet the formalized and elegant single combat of later centuries. The thirteenth-century tournament was a social occasion, but of a rough, purely masculine type. It provided an opportunity for the meeting of the most active members of the baronage of England, and this aspect had particular political importance during the reign of Henry III. Henry was one of the least warlike of the medieval English kings, and his brother Richard of Cornwall was equally uninterested in military affairs. Instead of the tournaments meeting by royal summons, and under royal patronage as they were so frequently to do in Edward's reign, they were called by the barons and attended by them, often in the teeth of royal opposition. The cleavage between the king and the barons, so acute throughout most of the reign, was widened by this royal disapproval of a favourite baronial sport.

But the social aspect was not the most important part of the thirteenth-century tournament. Just as the real reason for a knight's existence was his prowess in battle, so the tournament existed primarily as a substitute and rehearsal for the manoeuvres of battle. The tournament was the training-ground of the young knight, and a refresher course for his elders. When Pope John XXII, in 1316, finally abandoned the church's policy of opposition to tournaments, one of the reasons he used to support his judgment was the difficulty of getting enough trained soldiers for the crusades without these essential practices.[1]

Since thirteenth-century tournaments were usually wild mêlées of opposing groups rather than individual combats, serious injuries often ensued. Thus in the tournament of 1257 in which the nineteen-year-old Lord Edward fought, in linen armour and with light arms, many noble knights were so badly battered that they never recovered.[2] Frequently the trouble arose, not from the knights themselves, but from the crowds of unruly squires who fought among themselves in the fashion of their elders, and even trounced the defeated knights if they got the chance. Then tempers were inflamed and, if the state of the realm was precarious, serious trouble might easily ensue. Thus Earl Simon refused his sons permission to tourney with Earl Gilbert of Gloucester in the spring of 1265 because of the danger to the peace. Yet even though the authorities regarded them with suspicion, a round of tourneys was considered essential seasoning for the young knight – perhaps the medieval equivalent of the grand tour. In 1260 the Lord Edward, John of Brittany, and the recently knighted Henry and

Simon de Montfort the younger went overseas to compete in a tournament. The chronicler carefully explains that this was the custom with young knights.[1] Edward, at least, seems to have spent almost a year on a circuit of tournaments, and in time developed a notable reputation.

By the middle of the century, a new variation on the tournament was developing, quite different in style, and even intention, from the mass mêlée characteristic of the first half of the century. This was the Round Table, first mentioned by Matthew Paris in 1252. The chronicler very carefully distinguished this Round Table from the usual kind of tournament, and described it specifically as "a military game".[2] Unlike the usual tournament which was fought with swords and was primarily military, the Round Table was "a social occasion, accompanied by various games, of which jousting with blunted weapons was one".[3] Some of the games sound a little odd to us; they included skipping, casting the stone, wrestling, dart-shooting and lance-casting.[4] All the feasting and special games seem to have served as the medieval equivalent of a major sports meeting, and aroused much the same fanatical enthusiasm.

The preachers were always unhappy about tournaments; both Jacques de Vitry and Robert Mannyng used them as a convenient way of illustrating all the seven deadly sins at once. They particularized, with considerable relish, the various ways in which a tournament could offend.[5] Naturally the games and banqueting that went with the new invention of the Round Table, with its conscious bow to the Arthurian legend, seemed to the more strenuous clerics merely a further incitement to temptation. However in this case, as in so many others, theoretical disapproval had little effect upon common practice.

Only one other outside sport is mentioned in the accounts – the game of bowls. The Psalter of Isabel of France illustrates a game of this kind, which seems related to the modern one. Apparently they played in teams and rolled balls across a green – in the Psalter's case it was a distinctly humpy green![1] John of Brabant also played bowls, and there must have been some betting on the outcome, as once the game cost him 12d and on another occasion 6d.[2]

Indoors, chess was originally linked with social standing. The more popular it became among the barons, the more it was adopted by the lower ranks of society who found it a delightful way to ape their superiors. Chess must have been quite widely played by all classes in the thirteenth century, as Louis IX of France found it necessary to prohibit the bailiffs and royal officials from playing chess and dice-chess, as well as the more plebeian games of dice.[3]

Chess, which had been learnt from the Moslems, came to Europe about the end of the tenth century. Naturally the two centres from which it spread were Italy and Spain, the areas where Christian and Moslem daily rubbed shoulders. Spain in particular showed an early enthusiasm for chess, and at the end of the eleventh century the doctor of Alfonso VI, the king of Castile, included a knowledge of chess among the essential knightly accomplishments.[4] This identification of chess with the upper classes continued; indeed the fact that Edward I was so good at chess was considered a mark of his kingly qualities.

Since chess at present has such a formidable intellectual reputation, it is interesting to find it was so widely played in the Middle Ages. But the Middle Ages knew two forms of chess: one that depended on intelligence and ingenuity alone to make the moves, and another simpler form played with dice. Also the game which the Christians learned from the Moslems was not as complicated as the modern one; in fact it was Europe that gradually developed chess to its present form. It was popular partly because the upper classes in the Middle Ages had a great deal of leisure to indulge in long-drawn-out games. After all a baron, when not away engaged in fighting or hunting, exercised only a supervisory control over his household; the practical requirements of daily life were carried out by others. Chess was an ideal pastime for the long hours.

The fact that chess was not restricted to men may have been another factor which helped to add to its popularity, especially among the young. The lady of the household and her daughters also knew how to play and, if the testimony of the romances is exact, a game of chess was a frequent manoeuvre for lovers. It provided a legitimate excuse for a young man and his lady to spend hours with their heads close together over the board. In *Jehan et Blonde* the author carefully lists all Jehan's accomplishments as a well-brought-up young squire, and describes how he used to play at chess, tables and dice in the countess's chamber with the ladies.[1] Indeed a delightful incident in the great German romance of *Parzival* suggests that the chess set could even serve a double function. When unarmed Gawan was unexpectedly attacked by a large rabble while dallying with a beautiful maiden, the chess set was the weapon closest to hand. It was so large that it hung from the wall by an iron ring, and Gawan used it as a shield while his redoutable lady hurled the heavy pieces at the attackers, felling those she hit.[2]

Chess is often mentioned in more sober documents than the romances so that there is unimpeachable witness to its general popularity. The preachers, always vigilant for the possibilities of temptation, denounced chess vigorously in the early days. By the thirteenth century their attitude had changed; although they were still suspicious, they regarded it as the most virtuous of the games. Nevertheless Robert Mannyng carefully warned that it should not be played before noon on Sunday, since at that time all the world ought to be at church.[3] Indeed the preachers even adapted the game of chess to moral allegory, for it easily lent itself to symbolism. James de Cessolis, a Lombard Dominican friar, wrote a treatise known, in its English version, as *The Game and Plays of the Chesse*.[4] This described the history and rules of chess, but then went on to detail the duties of each state in life, arranged according to the moves of the various pieces. This allegory was extraordinarily popular, and was translated into all the usual European languages, and even into Greek.[1] Most of the storytellers of later centuries, including the Goodman of Paris, pillaged it for appropriate tales.[2]

Several of the household accounts of the time bear witness to the popularity of chess, and sometimes to the elegance of the chess sets. No English set was quite as rare as the one sent to St Louis at Acre by the Old Man of the Mountain, chief of the Assassins of Syria; it was of crystal and amber with filigree of gold.[3] However King Edward had two sets; one of jasper and crystal, and the other of ivory.[4] Bogo de Clare also had his own chess set, but probably only one for he carefully had it sent on to his manor of Thatcham to await his arrival there.[5] John of Brabant, who appears to have been consistently unlucky at games, lost 2s when he played chess at Christmas-time.[6]

Besides chess, both tables and merels were popular. Tables was a kind of backgammon, for which the board was often made on the reverse of the chess board, and merels resembled an elaborate tic-tac-toe. Both of them were games of chance played with dice. Dice were also used in other games of chance whose names no longer convey any meaning, and gambling was frequent. The moralists' impassioned denunciations were ineffectual; the quantity of sermons on the subject, and the wide range of illustrative stories used to point the moral, show that gambling was common to all ranks of society, students as well as magnates, clerics as well as laymen. Bogo de Clare, for example, had 3s to play at dice on Whitsun 1285.[7] This was a trifling sum for such a wealthy cleric, but the poet Rutebeuf put into despairing poetry the catastrophic effect of dice on poor men. Complaints about the seasons were a recognized literary formula of the time, but Rutebeuf's bitter denunciation of the winter cold, because the dice had robbed him of all his garments, has a more than conventional vividness.[8] The poet speaks for the submerged and voiceless multitude for whom dice were not a casual amusement but a trap in the desperate struggle for survival.

Books and playing-cards were not thirteenth-century amusements. Cards did not become known in Europe until the fourteenth century, and the laity normally possessed only books of devotion such as psalters and breviaries. Many of these had illuminated borders whose secular drawings must have served as a constant distraction from the sober religious text. The countess of Leicester ordered two hundred and forty leaves of the finest parchment for a breviary for her daughter; these cost 10s, and the writing at Oxford a further 14s, but there is no mention of any illumination.[1] The cleric of importance, or the scholar, might have a library composed of relatively few volumes for practical use. The Master of Sherborne Hospital had several service-books, a martyrology, books of saints' lives, a Sarum custumary, a book of medicine, Archbishop Stephen's moral compilations on Isaias and the twelve prophets, a glossed psalter, and a glossed epistles of St Paul.[2] This was really a fair-sized collection, but there is nothing here for amusement. Even King Henry, whose tastes seem to have been rather more literary than was usual in a thirteenth-century king or baron, seems to have had only one great book of romances, which was carefully bound with clasps, hasps, and silver nails.[3] Romances and stories more commonly passed by word of mouth, for story-tellers had the long memories of the almost illiterate. Such tales, songs and jokes enlivened dinner and supper, the great social events of the day. Sometimes the company entertained itself; sometimes they were amused by minstrels, the professional entertainers of the age.

There were many different kinds of minstrel, a class which included indiscriminately serious musicians, acrobats, and jugglers, as well as the professional story-tellers. A penitential of the end of the thirteenth century dealt very harshly with the minstrels, dividing them into three types, and damning most of them without question. The only class the author of the penitential considered allowable were those dignified entertainers who sang the deeds of great men and the lives of the saints, and "other such useful things" so as to bring solace to men in their troubles.[1] These men were universally respected and admired, and were popular among the serious clerics and the more sedate barons.

From the testimony of the accounts, it would seem that most of the minstrels were not the sober chanters of great deeds, but rather belonged to a class deplored by the moralists. These light fellows followed the courts of the magnates, told scurrilous stories and were useful to no one, the penitential declared pompously.[2] Despite these harsh words, many of the preachers had considerable respect for the minstrels' sharp wit, even when it was irreverent. Jacques de Vitry told the story of the minstrel who had taught his horse to fall to its knees whenever its owner said *Flectamus genua*, the phrase so commonly heard in the liturgy. When the minstrel said *Levate*, the horse would get up again. The minstrel used to amuse himself by offering the horse for sale; when the would-be purchaser had mounted the horse to try its paces, the owner would wait till they came to a very muddy place in the middle of the market. Then he would suddenly shout *"Flectamus genua"*, and the horse would sink into the mud with its unsuspecting rider until his master said *Levate*.[3] Sometimes royal jesters pushed their licence too far and suffered the royal wrath because of their unflattering conclusions. Most of the stories of the minstrels exhibit their wry attitude to life, which must have served as a welcome counterbalance to the excessive and easy emotionalism of all classes and both sexes. The typical attitude of a minstrel is best illustrated by the story of one who was in a tempest at sea. While his shipmates wept and called upon God to avert the shipwreck, the minstrel calmly ate great quantities of salt meat. His companions questioned his peculiar behaviour, but he replied calmly: "Never have I had so much water to drink as I shall have today, and therefore it behooves me to eat salt meat."[1]

The most complete account of the various types of minstrels is the roll of payments made at the great Pentecost feast of 1306 when Edward I's eldest son was knighted. Payments were listed for one hundred and seventy-five minstrels, not all of whom belonged to the royal court. Many of them must have converged on Westminster for the occasion, hoping to turn a few pennies on a day when the virtue of largess, which they considered the queen of all virtues, was likely to be most in evidence. There were even a few women among these minstrels, including one with the delightful name of "Pearl in the Egg".[2]

The ability to play a musical instrument was part of the stock in trade of many minstrels. The medieval vocabularies, as well as the encyclopedic treatises, give long lists of instruments, but without any distinguishing features so that many of them are difficult, if not impossible, to identify. Among the more usual are the viols, the citherns, the organs – at this time a small portable type – the drums, the cymbals, the timbrels, and even the bones.[3] The harper was the most respected instrumentalist of all, partly because of his biblical associations. Such a severe prelate as Robert Grosseteste had his own harper, and even gave him the chamber next to his own. When Robert Mannyng approvingly told this tale, he added the encouraging statement that:

> Virtue of the harp through skill and might
> Will destroy the fiend's might.[4]

Harpers were highly praised by laymen too. As early as 1183, the earl of Gloucester rewarded his harper with a grant of land in Bristol, for the nominal annual rent of a full dish of beans on St John's day.[5]

Once again the account of the countess of Leicester shows the abnormal nature of the days of worry and battle in the spring and summer of 1265; no such light matter as payment for minstrels or musicians appears in it. All the same it is an accepted item in most of the other contemporary accounts. Bishop Swinfield recorded several payments to minstrels and jugglers when he came to London, as well as to the more dignified harpers and a player of the viol. The London minstrels received from 1s to 3s, but when some country minstrels appeared to entertain the bishop when he was visiting at Monkton, they were rewarded at country prices – 1d each.[1] Bogo de Clare, as was proper for a wealthy cleric, had a harper as a regular member of his household, and also paid other jesters and actors on occasion.[2] The frequent travels of John of Brabant made him part of the company at many great feasts, and he then rewarded the minstrels at an average rate of 2s to 3s.[3] Indeed, the accounts bear out Rutebeuf's poetic statement that the minstrels flocked to feast or marriage; at the very least they were assured of a rich meal, and they stood the chance of gaining money or even a new patron. Often they would loudly demand patronage or money as their right in justice.[4] Despite their complaints and exorbitant demands, the minstrels added a welcome colour, gaiety, and diversion to the placid round of everyday life.

Another amusement was dancing, whether it was staged by the minstrels or by the company itself. Many of the minstrels' dances were acrobatic in character, such as those performed by the two Saracen dancing girls of Frederick II for the amusement of Richard of Cornwall. They were truly accomplished acrobats, for the girls danced on two balls while singing and playing the cymbals. Richard must have been enormously impressed by this Italian experience on his trip home from his crusade, for when he returned to England he gave a vivid account of the entertainment to Matthew Paris. The chronicler enlivened his report of the incident with a marginal drawing of the dancers balanced on a green sphere.[5]

The preachers did not approve of the dancing of minstrels,

but they deplored even more the popular dancing which marked all festive occasions. These round dances, in which the participants held hands and sung and circled, were known as *caroles*, and the word described the dances as well as the songs. Thomas of Cantimpre* brought forward an unusual reason to explain his disapproval of dancing: he declared that it was obviously evil because the dancers circled to the left like the damned.[1] Jacques de Vitry also regarded dancing as the devil's work, but the very violence of contemporary denunciations implies that dancing was widespread and very popular. Thomas of Cantimpre was sufficiently realistic to recognize the popular enjoyment of dancing, and even admitted that it was at least partially excusable to have dances at weddings. With the usual jaundiced approach to marriage of the medieval cleric he said grudgingly:

It is right for those folk thus to have the consolation of a moderate joy, who have joined together in the laborious life of matrimony. For according to the vulgar proverb, that man is worthy to have a little bell hung on a golden chain around his neck, who hath not repented of taking a wife before the year is out.[2]

Such simple and inexpensive amusements do not appear in the accounts, and indeed the occasional references to other games played, many of which have now been relegated to the children, can be very puzzling. Even an important household might amuse itself at times in many of the same ways as those the Goodman of Paris mentioned in one of his moral tales for his young wife:

---

* Thomas of Cantimpre was a brilliant preacher of good family, whose father had fought under Richard I in the Holy Land. Impressed by Jacques de Vitry's preaching, he became a Dominican c. 1231. His best-known work, *Bonum Universale de Apibus*, c. 1260, is a treatise on vices and virtues by analogy with the life of the bee, and is full of historical and personal stories.

Some ladies they found talking, others playing at *bric*,* others at hot cockles, others at "pinch me" ... others who had supped together were singing songs and telling fables and tales and asking riddles; others were in the road with their neighbours playing at blindman's buff and at *bric*, and so likewise at other games.[1]

The children must have shared in these games, but they also had their own toys, although these were seldom expensive enough to find their way into the accounts or the catalogues. The whipping top of the travelling pedlar,[2] or the "small cart bought for the lord's use as a plaything, 7d" are random examples of a much larger class. The toy cart had been purchased for Henry, King Edward's little son, and the account is precise enough to show that, like most other little boys' toys in the centuries before and since, it was soon broken.[3]

Finally there were the domestic animals, the dogs and the cats, as well as more extraordinary pets such as magpies and monkeys. There were many kinds of dogs with different functions: the fierce watch-dog, who was set free at night to attack any thieves, the dignified hunting-dogs and grey-hounds, the pampered little lap-dogs. Ladies frequently carried these with them, on their arm, and fed them with morsels from their own dish at the table. Not surprisingly, this habit was deplored by the writers on etiquette, who vainly insisted that it was impolite to pat dogs or cats while at the table.[4]

Cats were more strictly practical, and must have been omnipresent because of the need for mousing. When Bartholomew the Englishman came to his description of the cat, he drew his picture from everyday observation. He talked of kittens, and how they could be led on to play with a straw; perhaps influenced by the memory of many mid-

* *Bric* was played with a little stick, either indoors or out, but its nature is unknown. 'Pinch me' was mentioned among the games played by Gargantua, but its point is also unknown.[5]

night awakenings, he recalled the horrid noises of fighting cats.[1] The countess's household must have regarded a cat as a necessity, because they had no sooner returned to Odiham in February than a cat was purchased, another was bought soon after their arrival at Dover.[2]

The magpies and the monkeys appear frequently enough in stories to vouch for their popularity, but they seem to have been a rather specialized choice. Monkeys especially were to be found in the households of great clerics, and Fitz-Stephen's description of Becket's luxurious journey through France mentions that each sumpter-beast had its accompanying ape.[3] Given the size of Becket's pack-train this would almost qualify as a menagerie. One of the northern chronicles, alluding to a bishop of Durham's practice of keeping monkeys, described it as being "the custom of modern prelates for occasionally dispelling their anxieties".[4] In any case, no matter what their anxieties, there appears no trace of either monkey or magpie having come to the attention of the clerk in these thirteenth-century accounts.

It was no part of the duty of the clerk of the account to list the activities which occupied the leisure of his lord or lady; these only came within his view when they were an expense. However because the household accounts were so exceedingly detailed, they contain frequent hints which may easily be amplified by the evidence of the works of instruction and the example-stories of the preachers. Together they form an unidealized picture of the ways in which a baronial household amused itself.

11

Conclusion

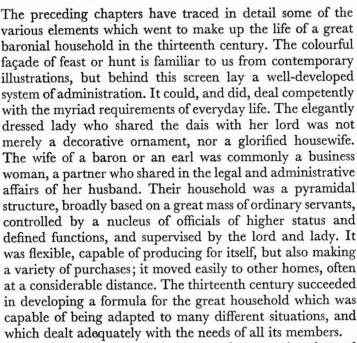

The preceding chapters have traced in detail some of the various elements which went to make up the life of a great baronial household in the thirteenth century. The colourful façade of feast or hunt is familiar to us from contemporary illustrations, but behind this screen lay a well-developed system of administration. It could, and did, deal competently with the myriad requirements of everyday life. The elegantly dressed lady who shared the dais with her lord was not merely a decorative ornament, nor a glorified housewife. The wife of a baron or an earl was commonly a business woman, a partner who shared in the legal and administrative affairs of her husband. Their household was a pyramidal structure, broadly based on a great mass of ordinary servants, controlled by a nucleus of officials of higher status and defined functions, and supervised by the lord and lady. It was flexible, capable of producing for itself, but also making a variety of purchases; it moved easily to other homes, often at a considerable distance. The thirteenth century succeeded in developing a formula for the great household which was capable of being adapted to many different situations, and which dealt adequately with the needs of all its members.

Our understanding of the history of any age is enhanced by a familiarity with that era's way of living. The patterns which guide men's lives are not merely constitutional or political; they are also, and perhaps primarily, social. Particularly in the Middle Ages, with its far more personal approach to the problems of government, the structure of social life had an important bearing on the development of political events. King and barons were dealing with problems which varied in magnitude, but which were essentially similar.

Apart from any possible connection with the stirring political events of the time, or any influence on them, the thirteenth-century household is interesting in itself, as an introduction to the life of the age. The household was a living organism, fulfilling a valuable function, and its meticulous accounting echoed the actual concerns of daily life.

Appendix

Appendix

The countess of Leicester's household roll has been the most important source for this book. The present translation of one of the membranes (the fourth) is a characteristic sample of this roll, which is the earliest private account for a baronial household to have come down to us. However there are other similar documents that have come down to us from the thirteenth century, though they come into a slightly different category. Many of them are likewise available in print, though still in the original Latin. Since these have also been frequently mentioned in the preceding pages, it has seemed appropriate to give some account of them.

It has already been noted that household accounts were a regular part of the administrative practice of the noble households of the thirteenth century. In fact they were such a standard matter that it is possible to find very early specimen accounts included in the manuscript collections of formularies which served as the reference manuals of the time. The specimen household account referred to in the text is part of a mixed collection of formularies compiled in the second quarter of the thirteenth century.[1] It lists in considerable detail, once in French and once in Latin, how the clerk should set up the household account, and gives characteristic expenditures for two or three days. This particular collection seems to have been acquired by William of Haseley, a monk of Westminster, who later gave it to his abbey.[2] This specimen account bears a close relationship to the style of accounting used by the clerks of the countess of Leicester, and contrasts quite sharply with the much more complicated system common by the middle of the fourteenth century. The later method is illustrated by a specimen account in a fourteenth-century formulary collection which belonged to the monks of St Edmund's.[3]

189

When Roger Leyburn campaigned against the rebels after Evesham, he submitted statements of his expenses to the Exchequer for repayment. The series of documents includes a daily account of his spending for his kitchen and stable as well as valuable information on military expenses. One membrane has been published covering the daily accounting during his service to the king between March 3 and June 6, 1267.[4] It closely resembles the daily accounting on the countess of Leicester's roll and provides a useful contemporary standard of comparison for the prices of available foodstuffs.

The most complete household account of the thirteenth century is that of Bishop Swinfield of Hereford. It has been printed in full for the year 1289–90, though unfortunately with all the manuscript contractions and abbreviations.[5] The bishop's household was naturally not exactly the same as that of a great secular baron, but there are fewer differences than might be expected. After all in the Middle Ages a bishop was essentially a baron with the usual accompaniments of a large household, and even his own knights and men-at-arms. Bishop Swinfield's more complete account helps to interpret the terms and items also mentioned on the countess's roll.

Another valuable series of accounts are those of Bogo de Clare, the rich and pluralistic cleric who was also the younger brother of the earl of Gloucester, the richest noble in England.[6] These accounts differ from those of the countess and the bishop because they include wardrobe as well as household accounts. The wardrobe account was a new development in the baronial household, copied, no doubt, from the increasing refinements of the royal accounting. The editor of Bogo de Clare's accounts does not print the household account, although he mentions items from it, but he does print the wardrobe accounts for 1284–6. The wardrobe account was essentially a summary, according to standard categories, of the miscellaneous expenses itemized daily on the household account, although it also contained more material about the superior officials and usually a statement of income as well as expenditure. For example the cloths used for Bogo de Clare himself, as well as for the various members of his household, were all listed together in tabular form as one of the sub-categories of the wardrobe account. It is a clearer method but does not provide the intimate view of day-to-day expenditure gained from the household accounts.

The other household accounts of the thirteenth century which have been published are all for children or close relations of the royal family. The most complete is that of young Henry, the son of Edward I, who died in 1274 at the age of seven.[7] It covers the period from February, 1273, to October, 1274. Because Henry was so young and his household was that of children – for it was shared by his sister Eleanor and his cousin John of Brittany – the account is almost a miniature and throws light on items unmentioned elsewhere. There is also a published account of the expenses of John of Brabant and Henry and Thomas of Lancaster in 1292–93.[8] John was married to Margaret, daughter of Edward I, and Henry and Thomas of Lancaster were the king's nephews, sons of his brother Edmund. This account is much more restricted than the others as the young men had no real household at this time, and merely gives details of their day-to-day personal expenses. Finally, some interesting excerpts from the relevant household rolls have been made by Mrs Green in her lives of Eleanor and Joanna, daughters of Edward I, but the rolls themselves have not been printed.[9]

The household roll of the countess of Leicester is Additional MS 8877 in the British Museum. It seems to have been taken to France by the countess when she left England, and was returned to England after the French Revolution. Written in Latin, it is a fragmentary roll, with neither proper beginning nor end. A note in French has been affixed to it

by a previous owner suggesting that it belongs to the year
1268, but internal evidence (the frequent mention of the
49th year, i.e. of Henry III's reign) proves conclusively that
it is for the year 1265. Physically, the roll is about twenty
feet long and eight inches wide. The thirteen membranes
which make up the surviving account are sewn together with
dogtooth stitches – the top of the following skin being sewn
to the bottom of the preceding. The roll is in reasonably
good condition, although it has been torn and mended in
several places, and the membranes show the occasional holes
which are characteristic of parchment. The handwriting is
mainly that of two clerks, Christopher and Eudes, who each
make a note in the margin where they take up the task.
By the evidence of the handwriting, Christopher was clerk
of the account when the surviving fragment begins. Eudes'
hand is neater and more legible than that of Christopher,
but they are both typical chancery hands of the thirteenth
century. At the beginning of the twelfth membrane it would
seem that a third clerk took up the task, as the nature of the
writing changes noticeably for the worse. However, there is
no marginal note to corroborate this.

My translation of the 4th membrane of the countess's
household roll relies on the printed edition published by
H. T. Turner in *Manners and Household Expenses in England
in the Thirteenth and Fifteenth Centuries*, a Roxburghe Club
publication of 1841. However, there has also been reference
to the manuscript itself to clarify any dubious points. A few
additions or modifications have been made to make the text
more easily intelligible to the modern reader. The date for
each day has been supplied in brackets, worked out from
the feasts originally named in the roll. On the dorse of the
membranes, the date has been supplied wherever there is
sufficient evidence. The marginal notes in the left-hand
margin have been moved into the main body of the text
immediately above the section to which they apply. The
figures for payment in the right-hand margin have also been

brought into the main body of the text, at the end of the entry to which they refer. Roman numerals have been put into Arabic, and fractions written out in Latin have also been put into Arabic numbers. Punctuation has been used according to modern forms. Titles have been capitalized, but otherwise capitalization too follows modern usage. Where the English version of a proper name is indisputable, it is given, otherwise names have been left in the form found in the MS. The MS varies between full names and initials for many individuals frequently mentioned, and I have followed the practice of the MS, but have standardized the spelling of any name used frequently.

Certain words in the roll are both commonly used and somewhat ambiguous. "*Panis*" has been translated as "grain" wherever a dry measure is given, but if there is only a purchase price, then it is translated as "bread". *Dominus* is a troublesome title, constantly used on many of the upper levels of the social scale and also as a courtesy title for clerks. It is translated here as the generally applicable "Sir" except in the case of the Lord Edward and the noblest personages. *Garcio* has normally been translated as "groom". *Mareschalcia* has been translated by "stable", rather than the more formal and less easily intelligible "marshalcy". Measurements have been abbreviated according to ordinary English practice.

Finally, I have not attempted to identify further the individuals named in this membrane, apart from those discussed in the previous chapters.

FOURTH MEMBRANE

On Saturday (April 25), for the Countess, the Abbot of Waverley, Sir Richard the Chaplain of Kemsing, and the above-mentioned; Grain, 7 bus. of "froille". Wine, 2½ sesters 1 gal. Ale, by purchase, 188 gals., 7s. 3d.; carriage, 3d. *Kitchen* 200 herring from stores. Fish bought, 8s. 6d. Butter, 6d. Eggs, 12d. *Stable* Hay for 31 horses. Oats, 2 qrtrs.   Sum, 17s. 6d.

On Sunday (April 26), for the Countess and Sir Richard the Chaplain of Kemsing, and Sir John, rector of the church of Catherington, and the household; Grain, 7 bus. Wine, 2 sesters 3 gals. Ale, previously reckoned. *Kitchen* 1½ oxen, 3 sheep, 16s. Calves, 3s. 3d. Hens, 3s. 8d. 2 kids from the castle stores. 150 eggs from rents. Eggs bought, 8½d. Milk, 2d. *Stable* Hay for 32 horses. Oats, 2 qrtrs. 1 bu.   Sum, 23s. 9¾d.

On Monday (April 27), for the Countess and Sir Richard Chaplain of Kemsing, and the household; Grain, 6 bus. of "froille". Wine, 2 sesters 3 gals. Ale, previously reckoned. *Kitchen* Fresh meat, previously reckoned. 1 ox, and ½ bacon from stores. 1 fresh sheep, from stores, and 2 kids. Eggs, 12½d. *Stable* Hay for 31 horses. Oats, 2 qrtrs. 1 bu.   Sum, 13½d.

Christopher
On Tuesday (April 28), for the Countess and the above-mentioned; Grain, 6 bus. of "froille". Wine, 3 sesters. Ale, previously reckoned. *Kitchen* ½ ox from the castle stores. 1 sheep and 1 calf, 3s. 3d. Hens, previously reckoned. 500 eggs, 17½d. Milk, 1d. *Stable* Hay for 36 horses, from stores. Oats, 2 qrtrs. 5 bus. from the constable's store.   Sum, 4s. 9½d.

For the dogs of Sir Henry de Montfort and Sir Guy for the 9 preceding days; Grain, 3 qrtrs. for 46 dogs.

On Wednesday following (April 29), for the Countess and the above-mentioned; Grain, 6 bus. of "froille". Wine, 2 sesters 3 gals. Ale brewed, 7 qrtrs. of barley and 2 qrtrs of "froille" oats. *Kitchen* ½ ox from the castle stores. Fish, 5s. For 700 eggs, 2s. 2¼d. *Stable* Hay for 30 horses. Oats, 2 qrtrs. from the Constable's stores. Sent to the friars of Oxford, by Seman, 5 lbs. of wax.

Sum, 7s. 2¼d.

On Thursday following (April 30), for the Countess and the above-mentioned; Grain, 6 bus. of "froille". Wine, 2 sesters. Ale, previously reckoned. *Kitchen* ¾ of an ox, 1 sheep from the castle stores. Fresh meat, previously reckoned. Calf, 16d. 3 kids from the Constable's stores. 2 lbs. of cinnamon delivered from the wardrobe for making sauce. Eggs, 14¼d. *Stable* Hay for 32 horses. Oats, 2 qrtrs. 1 bu. from the Constable's stores.

Sum, 2s. 6¼d.

Here we have taken from oats bought by the Constable. On Friday following (May 1), for the Countess and the above-mentioned; Grain, 5 bus. of "froille". Wine, 2½ sesters; sent to J. de Mucia, 1 sester, 18 loaves. Ale, previously reckoned. *Kitchen* 300 herring from the castle stores. Fish, 9s. 9d. Eggs, 12d. *Stable* Hay for 32 (horses). Oats, 2 qrtrs. 2 bus. from the Constable's purchase. Sent to J. de Mucia, 1 lb. of wax.

Sum, 10s. 9d.

On Saturday following (May 2), for the Countess and the above-mentioned; Grain, 5 bus. of "froille". Wine, 2 sesters 3 gals. Ale, previously reckoned. *Kitchen* 300 herring from the castle stores. Fish, 3s. 6d. For 600 eggs, 22½d. *Stable* Hay for 30 horses. Oats, 1 qrtr. 7 bus. from the Constable's purchase.

Sum, 5s. 4½d.

On Sunday following (May 3), for the Countess and

the above-mentioned; Grain, 6 bus. of "froille". Wine, 3 sesters. Ale, previously reckoned. *Kitchen* 1 ox and 1 pork from the castle stores; item, for 1 ox, 3 sheep, and 3 calves bought, 15s. 10d. Poultry, 5s. For 400 eggs, 15d. Milk for the week, 9 gals. from the castle. *Stable* Hay for 30 horses. Oats, 2 qrtrs. 1 bu. from the Constable's purchase. For 4 geese bought, 16d.   Sum, 23s. 5d.

On Monday following (May 4), for the Countess and the above-mentioned; Grain, 6 bus. of "froille". Wine, 3 sesters; taken with Seman, ½ sester. Ale, previously reckoned. *Kitchen* Meat and hens previously reckoned, and 1 fresh ox, from the castle stores. 300 eggs, 11¼d. *Stable* Hay for 36 horses. Oats, 2 qrtrs. 3 bus., from the Constable's purchase.   Sum, 11¼d.

For the wages of the grooms, as appears on the back, 15s. 2d. Grain for the poor for 8 days, ½ qrtr., and 13 gals. of ale. Grain for the dogs for 10 days, 3 qrtrs.
          Sum, 15s. 2d.

On Wednesday following (May 6), for the Countess and the above-mentioned; Grain, 6 bus. of "froille". Wine, 2½ sesters ½ gal. Ale, previously reckoned. *Kitchen* Fish, 6s. 11d. Calf, 12d. For 400 eggs, 15d. Cheese for tarts, 9d. 50 herring from stores. *Stable* Hay for 36 horses. Oats, 2 qrtrs. 3 bus. from the Constable's purchase.
          Sum, 9s. 8d.

On Thursday following (May 7), for the Countess and the above-mentioned; Grain, 6 bus. of "froille". Wine, 2 sesters 3 gals. Ale, for 36 gals., 17d. *Kitchen* For 1 ox and 1 sheep, 7s. Calf, 10d. Hens, 2s. 6d. For 300 eggs, 11¼d. *Stable* Hay for 36 horses. Oats, 2 qrtrs. 2 bus. from the Constable's purchase. Wax, from Friday the feast of St. Mark (April 24)* until now, 13 lbs.; for the chapel, 3 lbs. ½ lb. of pepper for the foals.   Sum, 12s. 8¼d.

* The clerk has mistaken the day of the week of the feast, which was actually on Saturday the 25th.

On Friday following (May 8), for the Countess and hers, and Sir R. of Havering; Grain, 5 bus. of "froille". Wine, 2 sesters 3 gals. Ale, for 160 gals., 10s., ¾d. per gal.; item, for 200 gals., 7s. 8d., ½d. per gal. *Kitchen* 250 herring from stores. Fish, 4s. 4d. Eggs, 6d. *Stable* Hay for 36 horses. Oats, 2 qrtrs. 6 bus. from the Constable's purchase. For the carriage of ale, 4d.   Sum, 22s. 10d.

On Saturday following (May 9), for the Countess and hers; Grain, 5 bus. of "froille". Wine, 2½ sesters; sent to Lady Catherine Lovel, 2 sesters; carried with Sir Richard the Chaplain, ½ sester. Ale, previously reckoned. *Kitchen* 100 herring. Fish, 12s. 1d. Eggs, 2s. 4d. 18 stockfish, for 3 days. *Stable* Hay for 38 horses. Oats, 2 qrtrs. from the purchase of the Constable.

Sum, 14s. 5d.

On Sunday following (May 10), for the Countess, Lady Catherine Lovel being present; Grain, 6 bus. of "froille". Wine, 4 sesters; sent with the above-mentioned Lady, ½ sester. Ale, previously reckoned. *Kitchen* Carcasses, 6s. 8d. Lard, 16d. Poultry, 5s. 8d. Eggs, previously reckoned. For the expenses of the dogs in taking 1 stag, by Michael of Kemsing, 6d. *Stable* Hay for 32 horses. Oats, 2 qrtrs. from the Constable's purchase. For 4 geese 14½d.   Sum, 15s. 2½d.

For 2 qrtrs. of malt wheat, 8 qrtrs. 2 bus. of malt barley, and 4 qrtrs. of malt oats bought from Lady Wimarc of Odiham by the Constable, soon after the Countess's arrival, 43s. 9½d. For the expenses of W. the Carter going to Porchester with 3 horses, to obtain 1 tun of wine, 3s.   Sum, 46s. 9½d.

Wax delivered to Sir Richard of Havering by order of the Countess, 20 lbs.; for the household, 3 lbs.

ON THE BACK OF THE
FOURTH MEMBRANE

By Gobion

For 5 housings for the foals of the Countess, bought by Richard Gobion, 4s. 2d.

For cart-clouts, grease, and small harness for the long cart, 20½d.

For the expenses of Robert de Conesgrave and 2 grooms with 2 horses, taking the robes of the King of Germany to Kenilworth, on Saturday after the Finding of the Holy Cross (May 9), 2s.

By Seman

For 1 new cart bought, bound with iron, and another repaired, by Seman, on Rogation Monday (May 11), 34s.

Paid to John de Mucia, on the same day, by the same Seman, 10s.

Given to the barber of Reading for coming twice to Odiham, with 1 horse hired for his use, to bleed a damsel, 2s. 8d.

For letters of the Lord King and the Countess carried to the Prioress of Amesbury, by the same, 4d.

For the expenses of W. the Carter seeking 1 tun of wine at Staines, 12d.

For 2 prs. of shoes and 1 pr. of hose, for the use of Robert de Valle, 16d.

For the expenses of Seman going to Portsmouth, 8d.

For the expenses of the same to Reading, 12d.

For the shoes of Petronilla the laundress, of the Easter term, 12d.

Given to Roger, the barber of the Lord Edward, on Rogation Monday (May 11), by order of the Countess, 14s. 4d.

For the expenses of Gobithesti going to the Earl, on the vigil of the Ascension (May 13), with a guide and rented mount, 2s.

On Ascension Day (May 14), given to the messenger of the Countess of the Isle, by order of the Countess, 12d.

On the following day (May 15), for the expenses of
Bolettus going to Pevensey, 8d.

On Saturday (May 16), for 2 grooms seeking a robe from
Joce, at London for 3 days, 8d.

For letters of the Countess carried to the Countess of the
Isle, 4d.

On Thursday after Ascension Day (May 21), given to a
certain groom coming from W. of Wortham, 6d.

On the same day, for the expenses of Bolettus going to
Pevensey, 7½d.

For 1 gilded plate bought at London, of a weight of
17d., for the use of the Damsel E. de Montfort, 2s. 10d.

Wages

Advanced to Perrot of the chamber on his wages of the
49th year, beginning at the feast of St Michael
(Sept. 29), 3s.

To Roger of the chamber, on the same, 3s.

For 2 carts hired from London to Kenilworth, with 2 tuns
of wine sent there by order of the Countess in Pentecost week, with the expenses of Colin going with
them, 18s. 6d.

Wages paid from the Saturday before the feast of the
Apostles Philip and James (April 25), on which day they
were set to wages, to the Saturday following, with both
days reckoned.

To 3 huntsmen of Sir Guy de Montfort, for 8 days, 3s. 4d.,
because the master takes 2d. a day, by order of the
Countess. To the huntsman of Sir H. of Almain and his
groom, 2s. 3d., for the master likewise, 2d. per day. To
2 grooms tending the foals of the Countess for the same
time, 2s. To two grooms for Sir Fulk Constable, 21d.
To 1 groom for J. Scot, 12d. To 1 groom for Andrew and
Thomas Mabile, 12d. To 1 groom tending the sick horses,
12d. To 1 groom for Michael of Kemsing, for 6 days,
9d. To 1 groom tending the greyhounds of the Countess,
for 8 days, 12d. To 1 groom of Brother J., for the same
time, 12d.

On Friday after Pentecost (May 29), to Gobithesti
going to Hereford to the Earl, 18d.

On the same day, for carrying letters of the Countess to Sir Richard of Kemsing and returning to Porchester, 7d.

For the expenses of 1 horse and a groom seeking the barber of Reading and bringing him back, 8d.

On Saturday (May 30), for Bolettus going to the Countesses of the Isle and of Lincoln, 6d.

On Sunday (May 31), for 1 groom going to Pevensey, 1d.

For 1 horse hired for the use of Dobbe the Parker driving the Countess by night to Porchester, 10d.

Given to the carter of Wintney coming with the Prioress's chariot to the same place, 18d.

To 2 grooms of the Abbot of Waverley coming with 2 palfreys, 12d.

To Picard, messenger of the Earl, on Wednesday after Trinity (June 3), 6d.

For the dinners of the grooms and the carters, 6d.

For the expenses of W. the Clerk at London, for 4 days in Pentecost week, 5s. 6d.

For 1 silk girdle for the use of Sir A. de Montfort, by order of the Countess, 3s.

For letters of the Countess carried to Kenilworth on Friday after Trinity (June 5), 5d.

For the expenses of Hicqe the Tailor going from Odiham to Kenilworth and returning to Porchester, on Trinity Sunday (May 31) for 5 days, with 14d. given for hiring 1 horse, 3s. 10½d.

For a sheath for the knives of the Countess, 3d.

For baths at Odiham, 3d.

For locks for the chests of the chandlery, 2d.

For the Countess's offerings from Easter (April 5) to the octave of Trinity (June 7), with the first day reckoned, 19s. 1d., by the hand of John Scot.

Porchester

For letters of the Countess carried to the Constable of Wallingford on Saturday after the octave of Trinity (June 13), 8d.

For Bolettus and 1 groom, going to Pevensey from Porchester, and returning, 2s.

For letters of the Countess carried to the Sheriff of Southampton on two occasions, 6d.

For those carried to Sir S. de Montfort by night, 8d.

Given to the groom of Brother Gregory on the feast of St. Barnabas (June 11), 12d.

For 1 groom carrying letters of the Countess to Raymond Ernald, 3½d.

For the offerings of the Countess, from the octave of Trinity (June 7) to the Monday before the feast of St. Botulph (June 15), 4s. 6d.

Paid by Seman to Hande, the groom from the bakery, dismissed on the same day, for 2 years wages, by order of the Countess, 7s.; and Roger de Lyons paid him 3s., and he is quit.

For 1 rouncey bought at Porchester, for the use of Amaury de Montfort, 30s.

For 1 messenger going to York, for the business of the same, 2s.

Given to the messenger of the Prioress of Amesbury, on feast of St. Barnabas (June 11), 12d.

On Saturday following (June 13), to Gobithesti going to Hereford from Lewes, 3s., by order of the Countess.

For 1 robe for the use of the same, by order of the Countess, 8s.

For 6 cinches for the palfreys of the Countess and the damsels, 7d.

Given to a certain messenger coming from Lourdes, 12d.

To the groom of Sir Hugh of Honull', leaving Bramber with 2 borrowed horses, 12d.

Notes

[*The abbreviations in the Notes are given in full in the Bibliography which is arranged under its various sections in alphabetical order.*]

INTRODUCTION

page

10 1. Painter, *Studies in the History of The English Feudal Barony*, 174. Denholm Young, *Seignorial Administration*, 9.

   2. Poole, *Obligations of Society*, 48–52. Sanders, *Feudal Military Service in England*, 68 n. 1.

13 1. Printed in *Manners and Household Expenses of the Thirteenth and Fifteenth Centuries*, ed. by H. T. Turner, intro. by B. Botfield. Roxburghe Club, 1841.

   2. Vernon Harcourt, *His Grace the Steward*, 102. The confused sequence of events has been carefully traced by Mr Vernon Harcourt, and is also discussed in *VCH Leicester* II, 83–6, 170, and the article by Levi Fox, "The Honour and Earldom of Leicester", *EHR* LIV (1939), 385–99.

14 1. Bemont, *Simon de Montfort* (French edition), App. XXXIV, 333.

   2. *CPR 1232–47*, 166, 419. *CPR 1247–58*, 5.

   3. *Lib. R.* III, 2.

   4. *CR 1231–34*, 310. Partition of Marshal lands in England and Wales, PRO, C 47 9/20.

Chapter 1: THE CASTLE AS A HOME

18 1. Gerald of Wales, *Itinerary through Wales*, 85.

20 1. *Lib. R.* III, 332.

   2. *Lib. R.* IV, 525.

21 1. Murray, *Le Château d'Amour de Robert Grosseteste*, 105–9.

   2. Br. Mus. Royal MS. 16 ii, f. 73.

22   1. *William Thorne's Chronicle*, 249.
     2. *Lib. R.* IV, 504.
23   1. Giuseppi, "The Wardrobe and Household Accounts of
        Bogo de Clare, 1284–86", *Archaeologia* LXX (1920), 29.
     2. Swinfield, 191.
     3. Salzman, *Building in England*, 175.
24   1. Giuseppi, "Bogo de Clare", 29.
25   1. *Lib. R.* II, 216, 266.
     2. *Lib. R.* IV, 507.
26   1. *Manners*, 8. See below, Appendix, 200.
     2. Hilda Johnstone, "The Wardrobe and Household of
        Henry son of Edward I", *Bulletin of the John Rylands
        Library* VII (1922); 402, 405.
     3. Dickinson, *Monastic Life in Medieval England*, 7.
     4. *William Thorne's Chronicle*, 249.
27   1. *VCH Leicester* IV, 345.
     2. *CPR 1232–47*, 419. *CPR 1246–58*, 5.
     3. Dugdale, *Antiquities of Warwickshire* (1676), 161a.
28   1. *CPR 1232–47*, 166. *CR 1234–37*, 386.
29   1. Clark, *Medieval Military Architecture* II, 336–46.
     2. *Lib. R.* I, 404.
30   1. Paris, *Chron. Maj.* V, 242.
     2. Colette Clark, *Home at Grasmere* (London, 1960), 301.
32   1. Toy, *Castles*, 79.
     2. *Manners*, 85.
     3. *Ibid.*, 48–50.
     4. *Lib. R.* IV, 323–4, 446.
33   1. *Lib. R.* I, 258.
     2. Paris, *Chron. Maj.* V, 509.
34   1. Wright, *Volume of Vocabularies*, 132.
35   1. *Lib. R.* I, 356.

Chapter 2: THE LADY OF THE HOUSE

38   1. Suchier, *Oeuvres Poetiques de Philippe de Remi* II, 11–13.
39   1. Paris, *Chron. Maj.* V, 336–7.
39   1. Pollock and Maitland, *History of English Law* I, 482.
     2. "Rules of St Robert" published in *Walter of Henley's*

Husbandry, ed. by E. Lamond, London, 1890. Grosse-teste also wrote *Regule ad Custodiendum Terrae*, a Latin version of the *Rules*. Probably both the Latin and the French versions were put out about the same time, c. 1240. There is also a single MS of *Statuta Familie* (published in *Monumenta Franciscana* I, App. IX, 582–6), a shortened version of much of the same advice. For the relationship of these various MSS, and also Grosseteste's treatise on etiquette, see S. Harrison Thomson, *Writings of Robert Grosseteste*, 148–50, 158–9.

41 1. Langlois, *Vie en France . . . d'après les Moralistes du Temps*, 24.

42 1. *Ibid.*, 195.
    2. *Ibid.*, 214.

43 1. *Ibid.*, 215.
    2. *Ibid.*, 195–6.
    3. *Ibid.*, 214–15.
    4. *Ibid.*, 235.

44 1. *Knight of La Tour Landry*, ed. by T. Wright, EETS (1906), 1–2.
    2. *Monumenta Franciscana* I, 264.

45 1. Bart. Angl. (Steele), 53.

46 1. *Ibid.*, 58.

47 1. Johnstone, "Henry", 388–9.
    2. *CR 1261–64*, 250–1. *CPR 1258–66*, 272. *CPR 1266–72*, 543.

48 1. "*Rules*", 135.

49 1. *Ibid.*, 5, 11, 19. See Appendix, 198. *CCR 1272–79*, 189.
    2. *Ibid.*, 12.
    3. *CPR 1216–25*, 441; *CPR 1232–47*, 2; *CR 1234–37*, 43. The last reference is *CR 1247–51*, 401. These references to Bartholomew de Crek I owe to the kindness of Dr C. H. Knowles.
    4. Br. Mus. Camp. Ch. III/1. This will, and the others quoted in this study, come from a group of thirteenth-century English wills studied by Rev. M. Sheehan, C.S.B., and listed in *The Genealogists' Magazine* XIII (1961), 259–65. Fr Sheehan has kindly loaned me his

transcripts of these wills, and my quotations are taken from the transcripts, which contain both MS sources and others previously published. However, I have given his references for the convenience of students.

5. *Cal. Inq. post Mortem, Edw. I* II, 713.

50   1. *Manners*, 47, 50, 62.

51   1. *Ibid.*, 73, 75, 67.

     2. *CR 1264–67*, 136. *Manners*, 74.

     3. *CR 1264–67*, 215–17.

Chapter 3: THE ORGANISATION OF THE HOUSEHOLD

55   1. T. F. Tout, *Chapters in Administrative History*, II, 182.

57   1. Midgeley, *Ministers' Accounts of the Earldom of Cornwall* II, 135, 69.

     2. Br. Mus. Add. MS. 8167, f. 132b.

     3. Johnstone, "The Wardrobe and Household of Henry son of Edward I", *Bulletin of the John Rylands Library* VII (1922), 384–420.

     4. *Manners*, 14.

58   1. J. Burtt, ed., "Account of the Expenses of John of Brabant and Henry and Thomas of Lancaster", *Camden Miscellany* II (1853).

     2. Alun Lewis, "Roger Leyburn and the Pacification of England, 1265–67", *EHR* LIV (1939), 193–214.

     3. *A Roll of the Household Expenses of Richard de Swinfield, bishop of Hereford, during part of the years 1289 and 1290*, ed. by John Webb, Camden Soc. old ser. LIX, 1853.

     4. Giuseppi, "The Wardrobe and Household Accounts of Bogo de Clare, 1284–86", *Archaeologia* LXX (1920), 2–52.

60   1. *Fleta* II, 243.

     2. Richardson, "Business Training in Medieval Oxford", *AHR* XLVI (1941) 259–80.

61   1. Crosland, *Medieval French Literature*, 148.

62   1. Jacques de Vitry, *The Exempla*, 166–7.

     2. Mannyng, *Handlyng Synne*, l. 5418.

     3. Vitry, 85.

63 1. "Rules", 133.
    2. *Lib. R.*, III, 335. *CR 1247–51*, 254.
    3. *Cal. Inq. post Mortem Henry III*, no. 647.
    4. *CPR 1258–66*, 528.
    5. *CPR 1247–58*, 61.
    6. *Cal. Inq. Misc.* I, nos. 611, 830.
64 1. *Fleta* II, 130.
65 1. Giuseppi, "Bogo de Clare", 12.
    2. *Monumenta Franciscana* I, 263.
    3. A. G. Little, *Grey Friars in Oxford* (Oxford, 1891), 186.
    4. *Monumenta Franciscana* I, 263.
66 1. Swinfield, 175 n. 46m.
    2. Br. Mus. *Guide to Medieval Antiquities*, 232–3.
    3. Swinfield, 175.
67 1. Stenton, *First Century of English Feudalism*, 70. App. XVII, 267–8.
    2. Turner, *Select Pleas of the Forest*, 13, 78.
68 1. Johnstone, "Henry", 391.
    2. Owst, *Literature and the Pulpit*, 36.
    3. *Manners*, 31, 41.
    4. Giuseppi, "Bogo de Clare", 17 n. 3.
69 1. See Appendix, 198.

Chapter 4: THE DAILY FARE

71 1. Transcript of Add. Ms. 8167, ff. 88–90 in *Neues Archiv* IV, 341.
    2. *Manners*, 47, 48.
72 1. *Fleta* II, 348.
73 1. Ross, "The Assize of Bread", *Econ. Hist. Rev.*, 2nd ser., IX, 336, 33.
    2. Rayner, "Reaping from Archives", *Archives* IV, 154.
    3. Postan, *The Famulus*, 20.
74 1. Ross, *op. cit.*, 333, 336.
    2. "Rules", 139.
    3. *Manners*, 14.
75 1. *Ibid.*, 29.
    2. *Ibid.*, intro., xxxvi.
    3. Swinfield, 171–2, 196.
    4. See Appendix, 201.

5. *Manners*, 67.

76 1. Coulton, *Medieval Garner*, 353.
    2. *Manners*, 16.17, 19.22.
    3. *Lib. R.* V, 162.

77 1. Rogers *Work and Wages*, 84.
    2. Lewis, "Roger Leyburn", 214.
    3. *Fifteenth Century Schoolbook*, par. 26.
    4. Johnstone, "Henry", 401.

78 1. *Walter of Henley's Husbandry*, 37, 31.
    2. Vitry, 70.

79 1. Salzman, *English Industries*, 260–1.
    2. *Fifteenth Century Schoolbook*, par. 30.
    3. *Fleta* II, 100.
    4. *Manners*, 14.

80 1. *Ibid.*, 16. The fishponds of Farnham appear to have been worked as late as the first World War.
    2. *De Antiquis Legibus Liber* (Camden Soc., old ser., XXXIV, 1846), 61.
    3. Beresford and St Joseph, *Medieval England*, 69.
    4. *Manners*, 13.
    5. *Chronicon Lanercost* (ed. by J. Stevenson, Edinburgh, 1839), 44.

81 1. Salzman, *English Industries*, 267.
    2. *Manners*, 14.
    3. *CR 1234–37*, 420.
    4. Lewis, "Leyburn", 212.
    5. *Ibid.*, 214.
    6. *Fifteenth Century Schoolbook*, par. 31.

82 1. *Manners*, 16, 19.
    2. *Goodman of Paris*, 275.
    3. Prior, "Weights and Measures", *Bulletin Du Cange* I, 88.

83 1. *Goodman*, 258.
    2. Bart Angl. (Steele), 105.
    3. White, *Medieval Technology and Social Change*, 76.
    4. Riley, *Munimenta Gildhallae* II, 534.
    5. Wright, *Volume of Vocabularies*, 136.

84 1. *Goodman*, 246.
    2. Lewis, "Leyburn", 212.
    3. *Manners*, 71.

4. E. Mâle, *Religious Art from the Twelfth to the Eighteenth Century* (New York, 1949), 67.

85   1. *Estate Book of Henry de Bray*, 49–50.
2. Giuseppi, "Bogo de Clare", 48.
3. Turner, *Domestic Architecture*, 140.

Chapter 5: THE SPICE ACCOUNT

86   1. Lopez and Raymond, *Medieval Trade*, 108–14.
88   1. Joinville, *Chronicle*, 182.
89   1. "Rules", 145.
2. Lewis, "Leyburn", 214.
90   1. Bart. Angl. (Steele), 108.
2. *Manners*, 14, 20, 71.
3. Giuseppi, "Bogo de Clare", 31, 43.
4. *Goodman*, 286.
5. *Ibid.*, 286–7.
91   1. *Manners*, 14, 20, 71.
2. Swinfield, 115. Giuseppi, "Bogo de Clare", 31.
3. *Manners*, 20.
4. Bart. Angl. (Steele), 103.
92   1. *Manners*, 14, 20, 71.
2. Swinfield, 115. Giuseppi, "Bogo de Clare", 31.
3. Swinfield, 115. Giuseppi, "Bogo de Clare", 31. The price on the bishop's account was 1s, on that of Bogo de Clare 18d.
4. *Goodman*, 287.
5. *Manners*, 21.
6. The most convenient source of information on the distribution and use of the various spices is W. Heyd, *Histoire du Commerce de Levant au Moyen Age*, 2 vols. Paris, 1885.
93   1. *Manners*, 14, 20, 21, 71.
2. *Goodman*, 263.
3. *Manners*, 14. Giuseppi, "Bogo de Clare", 32.
4. *Lib. R.* IV, 162.
94   1. Freeman, *Herbs for the Medieval Household*, 8.
2. *Manners*, 71.
3. Swinfield, 115.
4. Freeman, *Herbs*, 6.

O

96 1. *Manners*, 14, 20, 71.
    2. Lopez and Raymond, *Medieval Trade*, 352.
    3. *Cal. of State Papers Venice* I, intro. cxxxix.
    4. *Manners*, 20–21. Giuseppi, "Bogo de Clare", 52.

97 1. Johnstone, "Henry", 411, 412, 413.
    2. *Ibid.*, 409, 419–20.
    3. *Goodman*, 295.
    4. Swinfield, 115, 116.

98 1. Rogers, *History of Agriculture and Prices* I, 456.
    2. *Ibid.*, 478. Lewis, "Leyburn", 212.
    3. *Manners*, 63.
    4. *Ibid.*, 14, 20.
    5. *Forme of Cury*, 14, 87.

99 1. Salzman, *English Trade*, 411.
    2. *Manners*, 71.
    3. Johnstone, "Henry", 408, 413.
    4. Lewis, "Leyburn", 212.
    5. Giuseppi, "Bogo de Clare", 32.

100 1. *Manners*, 21.
    2. Stenton, *English Feudalism*, 71.
    3. See Appendix, 196.
    4. "Rules", 145.
    5. Swinfield, 115–16.

101 1. Rogers, *History of Agriculture and Prices* I, 445, 415.
    2. *Lib. R.* IV, 93.

Chapter 6: WINE AND BEER

102 1. Bart. Angl. Bk. VI, ch. 21.
    2. Bart. Angl. (Steele), 113.
    3. Johnstone, "Henry", 402.
    4. Bart. Angl., Bk. XIX, chs. 61–9.

103 Midgeley, *Ministers' Accounts* I, 31, 39, 40.
    2. *Manners*, 20.
    3. *Lib. R.* IV, 502. Midgeley, *Ministers' Accounts* I, 31.
    4. Swinfield, 77.
    5. Rutebeuf, *Oeuvres* I, 505–6.

104 1. Salimbene, *Cronica* I, 314–15. trans. in Coulton, *Social Life*, 29–30.

2. Swinfield, 59.

3. Midgeley, *Ministers' Accounts*, I, 45, 132, 48.

105 1. Renouard, "Le Grand Commerce des Vins", *Revue Historique* CCXXI, 273.

107 1. Salzman, *English Trade*, 383.

108 1. Carus-Wilson, "English Wine Trade", *Medieval Merchant Venturers*, 271 n. 1.

2. Renouard, *op. cit.*, and Carus-Wilson, *op. cit.*, and M. K. James, "Anglo-Gascon Wine Trade", *Econ. Hist. Rev.*, 2nd ser., IV, are the sources for this discussion.

3. *Fleta* II, 130.

4. *CR 1247–51*, 3–4.

109 1. *Ibid.*, 459.

2. *CR 1254–56*, 376.

3. Rogers, *Work and Wages*, 134–35.

4. *Manners*, 14.

110 1. *Ibid.*, 82–3.

2. *Fleta* II, 120.

3. Prior, "Weights and Measures", 152–3.

111 1. *CR 1247–51*, 274.

2. Sigerist, *Earliest Printed Book on Wine*, 40.

3. *Ibid.*, 41.

4. Migne, *Patrologia*, CCVII, 47; trans. in Coulton, *Medieval Garner*, 129.

112 1. "Rules", 145.

2. *Lib. R.* IV, 122.

3. Bateson, *Medieval England*, 314.

4. *Manners*, 22, 69, 76–7. See Appendix, 197.

5. *Ibid.*, 13, 16, 20. See Appendix, 196–7.

113 1. Fitzstephen, *Materials for the History of Thomas Becket* III (Rolls Series, 1878), 27; trans. in Coulton, *Medieval Garner*, 431.

2. Gerald of Wales, *Autobiography*, 71.

3. *Fleta* II, 118.

114 1. Cesarius of Heisterbach, *Dialogue of Miracles* II, 198–9.

2. *Manners*, 8.

3. *Ibid.*, 40.

115 1. *Ibid.*, 58–9.

2. Lewis, "Leyburn", 211.
3. Wells MSS, *Hist. MSS Commission X*, pt. III, 161.

Chapter 7: COOKING AND SERVING OF MEALS

117　1. *Luttrell Psalter*, f. 206b–207.
118　1. *Monumenta Franciscana* I, 170.
　　2. Wright, *Volume of Vocabularies*, 132. *Fleta* II, 248.
　　3. *Forme of Cury*, 11.
　　4. *Ibid.*
　　5. *Ibid.*, 58.
　　6. *Ibid.*, 54.
119　1. *Goodman*, 262.
　　2. Mannyng, ll. 7246–59.
　　3. Vitry, 2.
120　1. Langlois, *Vie en France*, 199.
　　2. Mannyng, ll. 7269–77.
　　3. *Ibid.*, ll. 7318–21.
　　4. "Rules", 137–41.
121　1. *Manners*, 21–2, 81–4.
　　2. Bart. Angl. (Steele), 61–2.
122　1. *Lib. R.* IV, 181.
　　2. Will of Peter Cosin, Br. Mus. Harl. Ch. 48 H 17.
　　3. *Wills and Inventories*, Surtees Society II, 9.
　　4. *Manners*, 8.
　　5. *Ibid.*, 9.
123　1. Giuseppi, "Bogo de Clare", 52.
　　2. See Appendix, 199.
　　3. *CR 1237–42*, 191. At the same time, the queen also
　　　　seems to have given Simon a silver pot, worth perhaps
　　　　16 marks, *Lib. R.* II, 100.
　　4. Giuseppi, "Bogo de Clare", 24, 34, 43, 32.
　　5. *Wills and Inventories*, Surtees Society II, 9–10.
　　6. Johnstone, "Henry", 406.
　　7. Swinfield, 60.
　　8. Will of Juliana Wyth, *Osney Cartulary* I, 411.
124　1. "Rules", 139.
　　2. *Manners*, 13.
　　3. Lewis, "Leyburn", 212, 214.
　　4. *Lib. R.* V, 145.

5. Bart. Angl., Bk. VI, ch. 24.

125 1. *Goodman*, 226–36.
2. Wright, *Volume of Vocabularies*, 173.
3. Bart. Angl., Bk. VI, ch. 24.
4. Gerald of Wales, *Autobiography*, 71.

126 1. Salimbene, *Cronica* I, 321.
2. "Rules", 139.
3. Bart. Angl., Bk. VI, ch. 24.

127 1. *Queen Elizabeth's Academy*, 17–31.
2. Supra, p. 71.

128 1. Swinfield, 35.
2. Morgan M 638, f. 17b.
3. Suchier, *Oeuvres Poetiques* II, 95.

Chapter 8: CLOTHS AND CLOTHES

129 1. Wykes, *Annales Monastici* IV (Rolls Ser., 1869), 158.

130 1. *Monumenta Franciscana* I, 294–96.
2. Johnstone, "Henry", 387–91.

131 1. *Lib. R.* II, 218.
2. *Lib. R.* I, 356.
3. Vernon Harcourt, *His Grace the Steward*, 82–3.
4. Will of Juliana Wyth, *Osney Cartulary* I, 412.

132 1. *Manners*, 25.
2. *Ibid.*, 85.
3. Carus-Wilson, "The English Cloth Industry", *Medieval Merchant Venturers*, 213 n. 1.

133 1. *Lib. R.* IV, 172.
2. *Manners*, 72.
3. *Ibid.*, 66.
4. Smirke, "Ancient Consuetudinary", *Archaelogical Journal* IX (1852), 77.
5. *Manners*, 74. Swinfield, 112.

134 1. *Lib. R.* IV, 337.
2. *Manners*, 25.

135 1. Heyd, *Histoire du Commerce* II, 697–701.
2. *Manners*, 25.
3. *Ibid.*, 85.
4. *Lib. R.* IV, 183–4.

5. Giuseppi, "Bogo de Clare", 15. Swinfield, 112, 184.

136   1. *Manners*, 10, 26.
2. Vitry, 38.
3. Johnstone, "Henry", 411.
4. Giuseppi, "Bogo de Clare", 38.

137   1. Inventory of Cecily House, PRO E 154 1/2.
2. *Manners*, 75, 73.
3. *Goodman*, 171.
4. Lopez and Raymond, *Medieval Trade*, 132.

138   1. Giuseppi, "Bogo de Clare", 36–7.
2. Swinfield, 112–13, 183.
3. *Manners*, 10, 18, 26.
4. Gerald of Wales, *Autobiography*, 128.
5. Joinville, Chronicle, 307.

139   1. *CPR 1258–66*, 502.
2. *Manners*, 65.
3. Johnstone, "Henry", 402.

140   1. Green, *Princesses of England* II, 330.
2. *Wills and Inventories*, 7–8.
3. Vitry, 77.

141   1. *Manners*, 10.
2. Burtt, "John of Brabant", 2.

142   1. Little and Douie, "Three Sermons", *EHR* LIV (1939),
13.
2. *Manners*, 75.
3. Vitry, 77.

143   1. *Lib. R.* IV, 120 and *passim*.
2. Coulton, *Medieval Garner*, 361–2.

144   1. Green, *Princesses* II, 330.
2. Mannyng, ll. 3338–51.
3. Riley, *Munimenta* II, 101.
4. Johnstone, "Henry", 406, 405, 407, 412.
5. *Manners*, 64.

145   1. Giuseppi, "Bogo de Clare", 20.
2. Johnstone, "Henry", 407, 403.
3. *CPR 1258–66*, 502.
4. Bart. Angl. (Steele), 42.
5. Fairholt, "Songs on Costume", 12.
6. Green, *Princesses* II, 313.

146 1. Lopez and Raymond, *Medieval Trade*, 132.
2. Burtt, "John of Brabant", 12–13.
3. Metropolitan Museum, The Cloisters, the treasury.
4. *Luttrell Psalter*, f. 63.
5. Evans, *Dress in Medieval France*, 201.

147 1. Joinville, Chronicle, 140.
148 1. Will of Bartholomew de Legh, PRO E–315, 42 (246).
2. Midgeley, *Ministers' Accounts* I, 132.

149 1. *Manners*, 55, 67.
2. Lewis, "Leyburn", 200.

Chapter 9: TRAVEL AND TRANSPORT

151 1. *Fleta* II, 248.
152 1. *Ibid.*, 129.
2. *Manners*, 10.
3. *Ibid.*, 69.
4. *Ibid.*, 50–5, 58–61, 71, 79. See Appendix, 198.
5. *Ibid.*, 57.

153 1. Vitry, 80–1.
2. Stenton, "The Road System of Medieval England", *Econ. Hist. Rev.* VII (1936), 4.
3. Salzman, *Building in England*, 383.

154 1. *VCH Warwick* II, 290.
2. Mitchell, "Early Maps of Great Britain", *Geographical Journal* LXXXI, 28–9.
3. *The Map of Great Britain known as the Gough Map*, intro., 16–20.

155 1. *Lib. R.* IV, 282.
2. *Wills and Inventories*, 8.

156 1. *CR 1247–51*, 261.
2. *Manners*, 3–4.
3. *Ibid.*, 42, 45–8.

157 1. Boyer, "A Day's Travel in Medieval France", *Speculum* XXVI (1951), 603.
2. *Manners*, 24. See Appendix, 198–9.
3. Hill, "King's Messengers", *EHR* LXI (1946), 315.

158 1. Swinfield, 170.
2. *Ibid.*, 128.

3. Giuseppi, "Bogo de Clare", 46.
4. Tout, *Chapters* II, 182.
5. Denholm Young, "Feudal Society, the Knights", *Collected Papers*, 63.

159
1. *Lib. R.* IV, 55, 64, 88, 95, *inter alia*.
2. *Ibid.*, 84, 496, 249.
3. *Ibid.*, 40, 259, 378, 448, 513.
4. Giuseppi, "Bogo de Clare", 34.
5. Madden, *Chapter of Medieval History*, 41–2.

160
1. Morgan M 638, f. 33b.
2. *Lib. R.* I, 288.
3. Burtt, "John of Brabant", 8.
4. Giuseppi, "Bogo de Clare", 53.
5. *Ibid.*, 21, 33.

161
1. Johnstone, "Henry", 407.
2. *Manners*, 20.
3. *Ibid.*, 20.
4. Fitzstephen, *Materials* III, 27.
5. Giuseppi, "Bogo de Clare", 54.
6. Green, *Princesses* II, 335–6.
7. See Appendix, 198.

162
1. *Luttrell Psalter*, f. 173b.
2. Rogers, *Agriculture and Prices* I, 543–6.
3. *Manners*, 15.

163
1. *Manners*, 39, 55, 64.
2. Robo, "Wages and Prices", *Econ. Hist.* III (1934), 25.
3. *Manners*, 39.
4. *Ibid.*, 13–14.

164
1. *Manners*, 63, 65.
2. Br. Mus. Harleian 4751, f. 69.
3. *CPR 1258–66*, 284. *Cal. Inq. Misc.* I, No. 881.

165
1. Owst, *Literature and the Pulpit*, 27 n. 10.

Chapter *10*: THE AMUSEMENTS OF A
BARONIAL HOUSEHOLD

166
1. Bazeley, "Extent of the English Forest", *Trans. R. Hist. Soc.* 4th ser., IV (1921), 160–2.

167
1. Paris, *Chron. Maj.* IV, 7.

168 1. Turner, *Select Pleas of the Forest*, 34, 98–9.
     2. Stubbs, *Select Charters*, 347.
     3. Turner, *Select Pleas*, 104.
     4. *Ibid.*, 161.
     5. *Ibid.*, 82.

169 1. Cox, *Royal Forests*, 61.
     2. Swinfield, 170, 195.
     3. See Appendix, 199. *Manners*, 40.
     4. Mannyng, ll. 3092–97.
     5. Coulton, *Medieval Garner*, 378.
     6. Vitry, 116.

170 1. Haskins, *Studies in the History of Medieval Science*, 263–4.
     2. Rosalind Hill, "Excommunication in Medieval England", *History* XLII (1957), 1.
     3. Burtt, "John of Brabant", 5, 8.
     4. *Lib. R.* IV, 52, 342, 346.

171 1. Madden, *Chapter of Medieval History*, 230–1.
     2. *Lib. R.* IV, 2.
     3. Burtt, "John of Brabant", 3.
     4. Quoted in Haskins, *Studies in Medieval Culture*, 111.

172 1. Swinfield, 169–70.
     2. *Ibid.*, 4, 10, 15, 30, 93.
     3. Bart. Angl., Bk. IX, ch. 12.

173 1. Denholm Young, "The Tournament in the Thirteenth Century", *Essays presented to F. M. Powicke*, 240 n. 2.
     2. Paris, *Chron. Maj.*, V, 537, 609.

174 1. *Flores Historiarum* (ed. by H. R. Luard, Rolls Ser., 1892) II, 456.
     2. Paris, *Chron. Maj.* V, 319.
     3. Denholm Young, "The Tournament", 254.
     4. Mannyng, *Handlyng Synne*, intro. xii.
     5. Vitry, 62–4. Mannyng, ll. 4576–4616.

175 1. *Psalter of Isabel of France*, f. 174.
     2. Burtt, "John of Brabant", 6, 11.
     3. Murray, *History of Chess*, 410 n. 50.
     4. *Ibid.*, 408 n. 42.

176 1. Suchier, *Oeuvres Poetiques* II, 30.
     2. Wolfram von Escehenbach, *Parzival* (trans. by Mustard and Passage, New York, 1961), Bk. VIII, 220.

3. Mannyng, ll. 1040–44.
4. Jacobus de Cessolis, *The Game and Playe of the Chess*, trans. by William Caxton from the French version of Jean de Vignay. Westminster, 1483.

177 1. Murray, *History of Chess*, 537–49.
2. *Goodman*, 99, 316.
3. Joinville, *Chronicle* 249–50.
4. Wardrobe Account 1299–1300, quoted in Murray, *History of Chess*, 449.
5. Giuseppi, "Bogo de Clare", 10–11.
6. Burtt, "John of Brabant", 3.
7. Giuseppi, "Bogo de Clare", 10.
8. Rutebeuf, *Oeuvres* I, 521–5.

178 1. *Manners*, 9, 24.
2. *Wills and Inventories*, 7–9.
3. *Lib. R.* I, 288.

179 1. Chambers, *The Medieval Stage* II, 262–3.
2. *Ibid.*
3. Vitry, 108–9.

180 1. *Ibid.*, 84–5.
2. Chambers, *The Medieval Stage*, II, 234–8.
3. Wright, *Volume of Vocabularies*, 137. Bart. Angl. Bk. XIX, chs. 133–45.
4. Mannyng, ll. 4756–57.
5. Stenton, *English Feudalism*, 266.

181 1. Swinfield, 148–9, 152.
2. Giuseppi, "Bogo de Clare", 11.
3. Burtt, "John of Brabant", 15.
4. Rutebeuf, *Oeuvres* II, 257–58.
5. Paris, *Chron. Maj.* IV, 147.

182 1. Coulton, *Medieval Garner*, 377.
2. *Ibid.*

183 1. *Goodman*, 102.
2. Fairholt, "Songs on Costume", 14.
3. Johnstone, "Henry", 400.
4. *Queen Elizabeth's Academy*, 27.
5. *Goodman*, 317.

184 1. Bart. Angl. (Steele), 165.
2. *Manners*, 2, 57.

3. Fitzstephen, *Materials* III, 27.
4. *Chron. Lanercost*, 114.

APPENDIX

1. B. M. Add. MS. 8167, ff. 132, 137.
2. Oschinsky, "Medieval Treatises on Estate Accounting", *Econ. Hist. Rev.* XVII, 58.
3. B. M. Harleian, 4971, ff. 26–9.
4. Exch. LTR Acc. E. 101/3 No. 9. m. 4 in Lewis, "Roger Leyburn", *EHR* LIV (1939), 211–14.
5. *Roll of the Household Expenses of Richard de Swinfield, Bishop of Hereford*, ed. by John Webb, Camden Soc., 2 vols., 1854–5.
6. M.S. Giuseppi, "Wardrobe and Household Accounts of Bogo de Clare, 1284–86", *Archaeologia* LXX (1920).
7. Hilda Johnstone, "Wardrobe and Household of Henry son of Edward I", *Bulletin of the John Rylands Library* VII (1922–3).
8. J. Burtt, "Account of the Expenses of John of Brabant and Thomas and Henry of Lancaster, 1292–3", *Camden Miscellany* II, 1853.
9. M. A. E. Green, *Lives of the Princesses of England*, II, London, 1849.

Bibliography

PRIMARY SOURCES

A. *Manuscript.*

ACCOUNTS
British Museum: Add. MS. 8877; Add. MS. 8167, ff. 132, 137: Harleian 4971, ff. 26–9.
ILLUMINATIONS
Morgan Library; M 638.
British Museum: Lansdowne 782; Harleian 4751.
WILLS
Cosin, Peter. British Museum: Harl. Ch. 48 H 17.
Creke, Margery de. British Museum: Camp. Ch. III/1.
Huse, Cecily. Public Record Office: E-210, 291. (inventory, PRO E 154 1/2).
Legh, Bartholomew de. Public Record Office: E 315, 42 (246).

B. *Printed.*

Bartholomaeus Anglicus. *De Proprietatibus Rerum,* trans. by Trevisa, Wynkyn de Worde, 1495. *De Proprietatibus Rerum.* Argentine, 1505. *Medieval Lore from Bartholomeus Anglicus,* ed. by Robert Steele, London, 1924.
Bosnier, C. "List of English Towns in the 14th Century", *EHR* XVI, (1901).
Burtt, J., ed. "Account of the Expenses of John of Brabant and Henry and Thomas of Lancaster", *Camden Miscellany* II, Camden Old Ser., 1853.
Calendar of Inquisitions Miscellaneous, vol. I (Henry III and Edw. I), 1916.
Calendar of Inquisitions Post Mortem, vol. I (Henry III) and vol. II (Edw. I), 1904, 1906.
CCR = Calendar of Close Rolls.
CR = Close Rolls.
CPR = Calendar of Patent Rolls.
Calendar of State Papers: Venice, vol. I (1202–1509), 1864.

Cesarius of Heisterbach. *Dialogue on Miracles*, trans. by H. von E. Scott and C. C. Swinton Bland. 2 vols. London, 1929.

Coulton, G. G., ed. *A Medieval Garner*. London, 1910. *Social Life in Britain from the Conquest to the Reformation*. Cambridge, 1918.

Crosland, Jessie. *Medieval French Literature*. Oxford, 1956.

EETS = Early English Text Society.

Estate Book of Henry de Bray, ed. by Dorothy Willis. Camden 3rd ser., XXVII. London, 1916.

Fairholt, F. W. "Satirical Songs and Poems on Costume", *Early English Poetry and Ballads*, Percy Society XXVII. London, 1899.

Fleta, ed. with trans. by H. G. Richardson and G. O. Sayles. Selden Soc. LXXII. London, 1955.

Forme of Cury, a Roll of Ancient English Cookery, ed. by S. Pegge. 1780.

Gerald of Wales. *Autobiography*, ed. and trans. by H. E. Butler. London, 1937. *Itinerary through Wales*, trans. by R. C. Hoare, intro. by W. L. Williams. London, 1935.

Giuseppi, M. S. "The Wardrobe and Household Accounts of Bogo de Clare, 1284–6", *Archaeologia* LXX (1920). London.

Goodman of Paris, trans. by E. Power. London, 1928.

Johnstone, Hilda, ed. "The Wardrobe and Household of Henry son of Edward I", *Bulletin of the John Rylands Library* VII (1922). Manchester.

Joinville, Jean de, Chronicle. In *Memoirs of the Crusades*, trans. by F. T. Marzials, New York, 1958.

Knight of La Tour Landry, Book of, ed. by Thomas Wright. EETS. Revised ed. London, 1906.

Langlois, C.-V. *La Vie en France au Moyen Age, de la fin du XIIe au milieu du XIVe siècle, d'après les moralistes du temps*. Paris, 1925.

Lewis, Alun. "Roger Leyburn and the Pacification of England, 1265–67", *EHR* LIV (1939).

Lib. R. = Calendar of Liberate Rolls, Henry III, vols. I–V 1216–67. 1917–62.

Little, A. G. "Three Sermons of Friar Jordan of Saxony", *EHR* LIV (1939).

Lopez, Robert S., and Raymond, Irving W. *Medieval Trade in the Mediterranean World*. Records of Civilisation, 52. New York, 1955.

The Luttrell Psalter, facsimile edition. Intro. by E. G. Millar. London, 1937.

Lyons, S. "Extracts from the Household Roll 18 Edward I", *Archaeologia* XV (1806). Trans. and notes by John Brand. London.

Manners and Household Expenses of England in the Thirteenth and Fifteenth Centuries, ed. by H. T. Turner. Intro. by B. Botfield. Roxburghe Club, 1841.

Mannyng, Robert, of Brunne. *Handlyng Synne*. ed. by F. J. Furnivall. Roxburghe Club, London, 1862.

The Map of Great Britain known as the Gough Map, intro. by J. S. Parsons, and *The Roads of the Gough Map*, by Frank Stenton. Oxford, 1958.

Ministers' Accounts of the Earldom of Cornwall, 1296–7. 2 vols. Ed. by L. M. Midgeley. Camden 3rd ser., LXVI, LXVIII, 1942–5.

Monumenta Franciscana = Letters of Adam Marsh, in *Monumenta Franciscana* I, ed. by J. S. Brewer. Rolls Ser., 1858.

Munimenta Gildhallae Londoniensis. Vols. I and III, Liber Albus; vol. II, pts. I and II, Liber Custumarum. ed. by H. T. Riley. Rolls Ser., 1859–62.

Nelson, William, ed. *A Fifteenth Century Schoolbook*. Oxford, 1956.

Neues Archiv der Gesellschaft fur altere Deutsche Geschichtskunde, IV. Hannover, 1879. Transcript of ff. 88–90, Add. MS. 8167, pp. 339–43.

Paris, Matthew. *Chronica Majora*. vols. IV and V, ed. by H. R. Luard. Rolls Ser., 1878–80.

Psalter of Isabel of France, described by S. C. Cockerell. London, 1905.

Queen Elizabeth's Academy, a Booke of Precedence, etc., ed. by F. J. Furnivall. EETS, Extra ser. VIII. London, 1869.

Report on the Manuscripts of Wells Cathedral. Historical MSS. Commission, vol. X, pt. III, 1885.

"Rules" = see *Walter of Henley's Husbandry*.

Rutebeuf. *Oeuvres Complètes*, ed. by E. Faral and J. Bastin. 2 vols. Paris, 1959–60.

Salimbene di Adam. *Cronica*, ed. by F. Bernini. 2 vols. Bari, 1942.

Sigerist, H. E. *The Earliest Printed Book on Wine*. New York, 1943.

Smirke, E. "Ancient Consuetudinary of the City of Winchester", *Archaeological Journal* IX (1852). London.

Suchier, H., ed. *Les Oeuvres Poétiques de Philippe de Remi, sire de Beaumanoir*. 2 vols. Paris, 1884–5.

Swinfield = Household Roll of Richard de Swinfield, Bishop of Hereford, 1289–90. Camden Soc. old ser., vols. LIX and LXII. 1853 and 1855. Ed. by John Webb.

Turner, G. J., ed. *Select Pleas of the Forest*. Selden Society XIII. London, 1901.

Vitry, Jacques de. *The Exempla, or Illustrative Stories from the Sermones Vulgares of Jacques de Vitry*, ed. by T. F. Crane. Folk Lore Society. London, 1890.

Walter of Henley's Husbandry, ed. by E. Lamond. Royal Historical Society. London, 1890.

William Thorne's Chronicle of St Augustine's Abbey, Canterbury, trans. by A. H. Davis. Oxford, 1934.

Wills and Inventories. Surtees Society II, 1835. Will of Master Martin of Holy Cross, Master of Sherborne Hospital.

Wright, Thomas. *A Selection of Latin Stories*. Percy Soc. VIII. London, 1842. *A Volume of Vocabularies*. London, 1882.

Wyth, Juliana. Will in *Cartulary of Osney Abbey* I; Oxford Historical Society, 89. Ed. by H. E. Salter. Oxford, 1929.

MODERN WORKS

AHR = American Historical Review.

Barraclough, Geoffrey, ed. *Social Life in Early England*. London, 1960.

Baldwin, J. F. "The Household Administration of Henry Lacy and Thomas of Lancaster", *EHR* XLII (1927). "Litigation in English Society", *Vassar Medieval Studies*, ed. by C. F. Fiske. New Haven, 1923.

Bateson, Mary. *Medieval England, 1066–1350.* London, 1905.

Bazeley, M. L. "The Extent of the English Forest in the Thirteenth Century", *Trans. R. Hist. Soc.*, 4th ser., IV (1921).

Beresford, M. W., and St Joseph, J. K. S. *Medieval England, an Aerial Survey.* Cambridge, 1958.

Boyer, M. N. "A Day's Journey in Medieval France", *Speculum* XXVI (1951).

British Museum. *Guide to Medieval Antiquities.* London, 1924.

Brieger, Peter. *English Art, 1216–1307.* Vol. IV of Oxford History of English Art. Oxford, 1957.

Brown, R. A. "Castles", *EHR* LXXIV (1959). *English Medieval Castles.* London, 1954.

Cambridge Economic History. Vol. I ed. by J. Clapham and E. Power; vol. II ed. by M. Postan and A. Rich. Cambridge, 1942–52.

Carus-Wilson, E. *Medieval Merchant Venturers.* London, 1954.

Chambers, E. K. *The Medieval Stage.* 2 vols. Oxford, 1903.

Clark, G. T. *Medieval Military Architecture in England.* 2 vols. London, 1884.

Cledat, Leon. *Rutebeuf.* Paris, 1891.

Cline, Ruth. "The Influence of Romances in Tournaments of the Middle Ages", *Speculum* XX (1945).

Cox, J. Charles. *The Royal Forests of England.* London, 1905.

Crisp, Frank. *Medieval Gardens.* 2 vols. London, 1924.

Crombie, A. C. *Medieval and Early Modern Science.* Vol. I. 2nd ed. New York, 1959.

Crosby, Ruth. "Robert Mannyng of Brunne, a New Biography", *PMLA* LVII (1942).

Denholm-Young, N. *Collected Papers on Medieval Subjects.* Oxford, 1946. *Seignorial Administration in England.* Oxford, 1937. "The Tournament in the Thirteenth Century", *Studies in Medieval History presented to F. M. Powicke.* Oxford, 1948.

Dickinson, J. C. *Monastic Life in Medieval England.* London, 1961.

EHR = English Historical Review.

Evans, Joan. *Dress in Medieval France.* Oxford, 1952. *Art in*

Medieval France, 987–1948. London, 1948. *Life in Medieval France.* London, 1957.

Faral, E. *La Vie Quotidienne au temps de St Louis.* Paris, 1938.

Farmer, D. L. "Grain Price Movements in 13th Century England", *Econ. Hist. Rev.*, 2nd ser., vol. X (1957–58).

ffoulkes, Charles. *The Armourer and His Craft, from the XIth to the XVIth Century.* London, 1912.

Freeman, Margaret. *Herbs for the Medieval Household.* New York, 1943.

Gras, N. S. B. *The Early English Customs System.* Cambridge, Mass., 1918.

Green, M. A. E. *Lives of the Princesses of England*, II. London, 1842.

Harden, D. B. "Domestic Window Glass; Roman, Saxon, and Medieval", *Studies in Building History*, ed. by E. M. Jope. London, 1961.

Hartley, D. *Medieval Costume and Life.* Intro. and Notes by F. M. Kelly. London, 1931.

Hartley, D., and Elliot, M. *The Life and Work of the People of England;* vol. I, from the year 1000 to 1300 A.D. London, 1931.

Haskins, C. H. *Studies in the History of Medieval Science.* Reprint ed. New York, 1960. *Studies in Medieval Culture.* Reprinted. New York, 1958.

Heyd, W. *Histoire du Commerce de Levant au Moyen-Age.* 2 vols. Paris, 1885.

Hill, M. S. "King's messengers and Administrative Developments in the Thirteenth and Fourteenth Century", *EHR* LXI (1946).

Holmes, U.T., jr. *Daily Living in the Twelfth Century.* Madison, Wis., 1953.

Houston, Mary G. *Medieval Costume in England and France.* London, 1950.

James, M. K. "The Fluctuations of the Anglo-Gascon Wine Trade during the Fourteenth Century", *Econ. Hist. Rev.*, 2nd ser., IV (1951).

Johnstone, Hilda. "The Wardrobe and Household Accounts of the Sons of Edward I", *Bulletin of the Institute of Historical Research* II, 1924.

Kelly, F. M., and Schwab, R. *A Short History of Costume and Armour*. London, 1931.

Lane-Poole, A., ed. *Medieval England*. 2 vols. Oxford, 1958.

London Museum. *Medieval Catalogue*. London, 1954.

Madden, D. H. *A Chapter of Medieval History*. London, 1924.

Mead, William. *The English Medieval Feast*. London, 1931.

Mitchell, J. B. "Early Maps of Great Britain; the Matthew Paris maps", *Geographical Journal* LXXXI (1933).

Murray, H. J. R. *A History of Chess*. Oxford, 1913.

Murray, J. *Le Château d'Amour de Robert Grosseteste, Evêque de Lincoln*. Paris, 1918.

Oman, Charles. *A History of the Art of War in the Middle Ages*. 2nd ed. revised and enlarged. 2 vols. London, 1924.

O'Neil, B. H. St J. *Castles, an Introduction to the Castles of England and Wales*. London, 1954.

Oschinsky, D. "Medieval Treatises on Estate Accounting", *Econ. Hist. Rev.* XVII (1947).

Owst, G. R. *Literature and Pulpit in Medieval England*. Cambridge, 1933. *Preaching in Medieval England*. Cambridge, 1926.

Painter, Sidney. *Feudalism and Liberty, Articles and Addresses*. Baltimore, 1961. *Studies in the History of the English Feudal Barony*. Baltimore, 1943.

Petit-Dutaillis, Ch., and Lefebvre, G. "The Forest", *Studies and Notes supplementary to Stubbs' Constitutional History*. Manchester, 1930.

Pollock, F., and Maitland, F. M. History of English Law before the Time of Edward I, 2 vols. 2nd ed. Cambridge, 1911.

Postan, M. "The famulus", *Economic History Review* supplements, No. 2.

Power, E. *Medieval English Nunneries, c. 1275–1535*. Cambridge, 1922. *Medieval People*. London, 1924. "The Position of Women", *Legacy of the Middle Ages*, ed. G. C. Crump and E. F. Jacob. Oxford, 1926.

Prior, W. H. "Notes on the Weights and Measures of Medieval England", *Archivum Latinitatis Medii Aevi (Bulletin Du Cange)* I (1924–5).

Quennell, M., and C. B. *A History of Everyday Things in England*, vol. I. London, 1945.

Rayner, M. E. "Reaping from Archives in an Archaelogical Famine", *Archives* IV (1960).

Renouard, Yves. "Le Grand Commerce des Vins de Gascogne au Moyen Age", *Revue Historique* CCXXI (1959). *Les Hommes d'Affaires Italiens du Moyen Age*. Paris, 1949.

Richardson, H. G. "Business Training in Medieval Oxford", *AHR* XLVI (1941).

Robertson, D. W. "The Cultural Tradition of *Handlyng Synne*", *Speculum* XXII (1947).

Robo, Etienne. "Wages and Prices in the Hundred of Farnham in the Thirteenth Century", *Econ. Hist.* III (1934).

Robinson, F. A. "Household Roll of Bishop Ralph of Shrewsbury (1337–81)", *Collectanea* I, Somerset Record Soc., 1924. (Note by H. Thompson on the household roll of Bishop Swinfield.)

Rogers, J. E. Thorold. *History of Agriculture and Prices in England*, vols. I and II. London, 1866. *Six Centuries of Work and Wages*. 5th ed. London, 1901.

Ross, A. S. C. "The Assize of Bread", *Econ. Hist. Rev.*, 2nd ser., vol. IX (1956–7).

Salzman, L. F. *Building in England down to 1540*. Oxford, 1952. *English Industries of the Middle Ages*. Oxford, 1926. *English Life in the Middle Ages*. London, 1926. *English Trade in the Middle Ages*. Oxford, 1931.

Seaton, Ethel. "Robert Mannyng of Brunne in Lincoln", *Medium Aevum* XII (1943).

Singer, Charles; Holmyard, E. J.; Hall, A. R.; *A History of Technology*, vol. II; the Mediterranean Civilisation and the Middle Ages. Oxford, 1955.

Stenton, Doris Mary. *The English Woman in History*. London, 1957.

Stenton, F. M. *The First Century of English Feudalism*. Oxford, 1932. "The Road System of Medieval England", *Econ. Hist. Rev.* VII (1936).

Thomson, S. Harrison. *The Writings of Robert Grosseteste.* Cambridge, 1940.

Thorndike, Lynn. *History of Magic and Experimental Science,* vol. II. New York, 1947.

Tout, T. F. *Chapters in the Administrative History of Medieval England,* vols. II and V. Manchester, 1937, 1930.

Toy, Sidney. *Castles.* London, 1939.

Turner, H. T. *Some Account of Domestic Architecture in England from the Conquest to the End of the Thirteenth Century.* Oxford and London, 1851.

Vaughan, R. *Matthew Paris.* Cambridge, 1958.

VCH = Victoria County History.

Vernon Harcourt, L. W. *His Grace the Steward and Trial of Peers.* London, 1907.

White, Lynn, jr. *Medieval Technology and Social Change.* Oxford, 1962.

Whitney, M. P. "Queen of Medieval Virtues, Largesse", *Vassar Medieval Studies,* ed. by C. F. Fiske. New Haven, 1923.

Williamson, J. A. *The English Channel.* London, 1959.

Wood, Margaret E. "Thirteenth Century Domestic Architecture in England", *Archaeological Journal,* supplement to vol. CV (1950).

Wright, Thomas. *The Homes of Other Days, A History of Domestic Manners and Sentiments in England.* London, 1871.

Index